MONSTER JUMBLE®

A Scary Good Puzzle Collection!

Henri Arnold,
Bob Lee,
Jeff Knurek, &
David L. Hoyt

TRIUMPH
BOOKS

Jumble° is a registered trademark
of Tribune Media Services, Inc.

Copyright © 2016 by Tribune Media Services, Inc.
All rights reserved.

This book is available in quantity at special discounts
for your group or organization.

For further information, contact:

Triumph Books LLC
814 North Franklin Street
Chicago, Illinois 60610
Phone: (312) 337-0747
www.triumphbooks.com

Printed in U.S.A.

ISBN: 978-1-62937-213-6

Design by Sue Knopf

CONTENTS

Classic Puzzles

Daily Puzzles

Challenger Puzzles

Answers

MONSTER JUMBLE®

Classic Puzzles

JUMBLE®

Unscramble these four Jumbles, one letter to each square, to form four ordinary words.

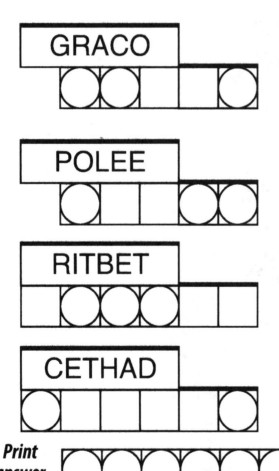

GRACO

POLEE

RITBET

CETHAD

I'm telling you, it's never been so hot!

You're crazy! Last winter was freezing.

It's not normal!

You're crazy! It's cyclical.

FOR SOME PEOPLE, GLOBAL WARMING IS A ---

Now arrange the circled letters to form the surprise answer, as suggested by the above cartoon.

Print answer here

JUMBLE®

Unscramble these four Jumbles, one letter to each square, to form four ordinary words.

KEEOV

YORNA

YENOLF

REMHIT

You're blocking the sidewalk. Do you have a permit?

A what?

I love it!

BUSINESS WAS GOOD, BUT THE POLICEMAN ONLY WANTED TO ----

Now arrange the circled letters to form the surprise answer, as suggested by the above cartoon.

Print answer here

JUMBLE®

Unscramble these four Jumbles, one letter to each square, to form four ordinary words.

BUCCI

ATBIH

PYSMIK

IDRONO

That's a big skull.

I wish I could ask him about his life.

THE ARCHAEOLOGIST WISHED THE CAVEMAN WAS STILL ALIVE SO HE COULD ----

Now arrange the circled letters to form the surprise answer, as suggested by the above cartoon.

Print answer here

4

JUMBLE®

Unscramble these four Jumbles, one letter to each square, to form four ordinary words.

LEMPI

GRPUE

DUGERT

ICOSAF

I'll cover some of the bare spots.

It will look beautiful.

WHEN THEY ADDED ORNAMENTS TO THE CHRISTMAS TREE, THEY ----

Now arrange the circled letters to form the surprise answer, as suggested by the above cartoon.

Print answer here

JUMBLE

Unscramble these four Jumbles, one letter to each square, to form four ordinary words.

RAWEF

DATPA

HOYLUR

CAZIOD

HE PUT UP SO MANY CHRISTMAS LIGHTS, THE NEIGHBORS WERE IN A ---

Now arrange the circled letters to form the surprise answer, as suggested by the above cartoon.

Print answer here " ☐☐☐☐ - ☐☐☐☐ "

6

JUMBLE®

Unscramble these four Jumbles, one letter to
each square, to form four ordinary words.

DUWEN

CRUCO

BEERKU

ROGFTO

When will we be ready to strike back?

Soon. I have everyone under my control.

THE EMPIRE WAS ABLE
TO GET ANOTHER DEATH
STAR BUILT QUICKLY,
THANKS TO THE ----

Now arrange the circled letters to form
the surprise answer, as suggested by the
above cartoon.

Print answer here

7

JUMBLE®

Unscramble these four Jumbles, one letter to each square, to form four ordinary words.

BACNI

APORE

DELODO

UGATOE

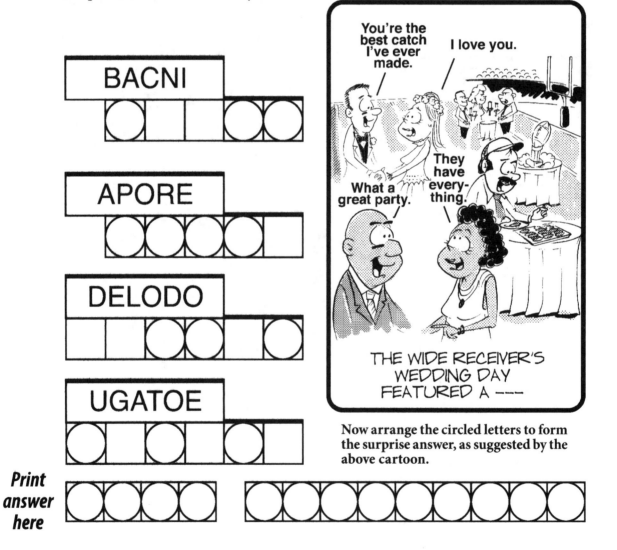

You're the best catch I've ever made.

I love you.

What a great party.

They have every-thing.

THE WIDE RECEIVER'S WEDDING DAY FEATURED A ---

Now arrange the circled letters to form the surprise answer, as suggested by the above cartoon.

Print answer here

8

JUMBLE

Unscramble these four Jumbles, one letter to each square, to form four ordinary words.

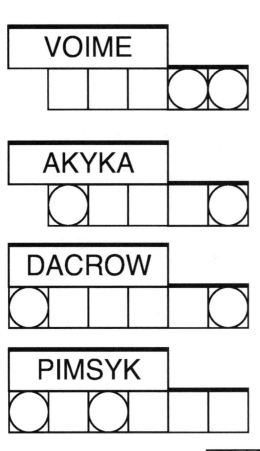

VOIME

AKYKA

DACROW

PIMSYK

Hyah!

I've never seen him so forceful.

YOGI AND BOO-BOO WERE TAKING KARATE LESSONS AND YOGI WAS IMPRESSED WITH HIS ----

Now arrange the circled letters to form the surprise answer, as suggested by the above cartoon.

Print answer here

JUMBLE®

Unscramble these four Jumbles, one letter to each square, to form four ordinary words.

TUMHO

FORFE

CAPTIM

YATNOB

It will be strong enough to withstand the pressures.

This would be too expensive.

You expect this to go 36,000 feet down?

HE PROPOSED A SUBMARINE TO REACH THE BOTTOM OF THE OCEAN, BUT HIS BOSS COULDN'T ---

Now arrange the circled letters to form the surprise answer, as suggested by the above cartoon.

Print answer here

10

JUMBLE®

Unscramble these four Jumbles, one letter to each square, to form four ordinary words.

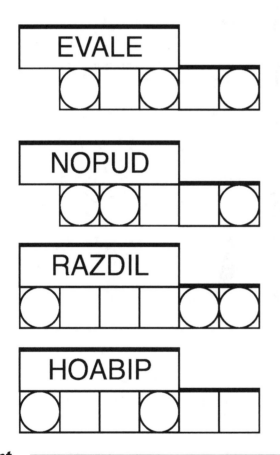

EVALE

NOPUD

RAZDIL

HOABIP

Perfect. This is going off without a hitch.

7,6,5...

I'm glad I didn't mess up.

NEW YEAR'S EVE WOULD BE PROBLEM-FREE, AS LONG AS SOMEONE ---

Now arrange the circled letters to form the surprise answer, as suggested by the above cartoon.

Print answer here

THE

JUMBLE®

Unscramble these four Jumbles, one letter to each square, to form four ordinary words.

DIMTA

CIYED

ROGNAJ

WORDYS

How do you shoot with this wind?

I designed these to cut through high winds.

HE MADE SUCH A GOOD ARCHER BECAUSE HE UNDERSTOOD ---

Now arrange the circled letters to form the surprise answer, as suggested by the above cartoon.

Print answer here

JUMBLE®

Unscramble these four Jumbles, one letter to each square, to form four ordinary words.

GREEV

SURCH

CANYEG

TETINN

I can't get it over the net.

It's all mechanics. I'll have you fixed in a jiffy.

THE TENNIS PLAYER WAS DOUBLE-FAULTING WAY TOO MUCH, SO HE WENT TO A ---

Now arrange the circled letters to form the surprise answer, as suggested by the above cartoon.

Print answer here

JUMBLE®

Unscramble these four Jumbles, one letter to each square, to form four ordinary words.

IDTOT

GODDE

DARCIN

CONHOP

Who can tell me what 36 plus 36 is?

36 24
+36 +24

The kids love him.

I'm glad we hired him.

THE SCHOOL'S NEW MATH TEACHER WAS A ----

Now arrange the circled letters to form the surprise answer, as suggested by the above cartoon.

Print answer here

14

JUMBLE®

Unscramble these four Jumbles, one letter to each square, to form four ordinary words.

CUJIE

ENVTE

CLORSL

LIFTEL

Here. I thought you may need a new hat.

Wow! That is so kind of you.

WHEN THE CLOWN HELPED OUT THE RINGMASTER, HE WAS A ---

Now arrange the circled letters to form the surprise answer, as suggested by the above cartoon.

Print answer here

JUMBLE®

Unscramble these four Jumbles, one letter to each square, to form four ordinary words.

GAMIE

TOTDI

SNUJTU

CANGEL

Welcome Jumble Society

How many people do you think are here this weekend?

I don't know exactly, but I think…

I think that's Jumble Jeff!

HE WASN'T SURE EXACTLY HOW MANY PEOPLE WERE STAYING AT THE HOTEL, SO HE ---

Now arrange the circled letters to form the surprise answer, as suggested by the above cartoon.

Print answer here " ☐☐☐☐☐ - ☐☐☐☐☐☐ "

JUMBLE®

Unscramble these four Jumbles, one letter to each square, to form four ordinary words.

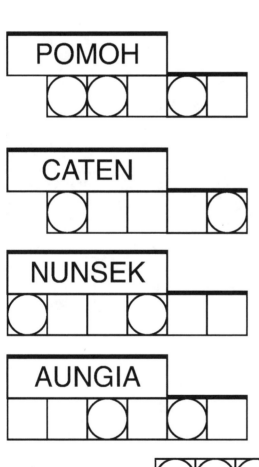

POMOH

CATEN

NUNSEK

AUNGIA

I call it the way I see it!

Well, you called it wrong. I was safe by a mile.

AFTER NOT BEING CALLED SAFE, THE BASEBALL PLAYER WAS ---

Now arrange the circled letters to form the surprise answer, as suggested by the above cartoon.

Print answer here

17

JUMBLE®

Unscramble these four Jumbles, one letter to each square, to form four ordinary words.

CONUE

BYRED

DENROV

ALUTOW

You have to believe, Peter.

When will you learn, Peter?

PETER PAN COULDN'T FIGHT CAPTAIN HOOK BECAUSE HIS PUNCHES WOULD ----

Now arrange the circled letters to form the surprise answer, as suggested by the above cartoon.

Print answer here

JUMBLE®

Unscramble these four Jumbles, one letter to each square, to form four ordinary words.

ZOGIM

LORTL

UNITYM

FLOSIS

Excuse me, Mr. Tolstoy. May I ask how you researched this?

Well. I'll start at the beginning. It's quite interesting.

IF YOU ASKED TOLSTOY WHY "WAR AND PEACE" HAD 1,225 PAGES, HE'D SAY IT WAS A ---

Now arrange the circled letters to form the surprise answer, as suggested by the above cartoon.

Print answer here

JUMBLE®

Unscramble these four Jumbles, one letter to each square, to form four ordinary words.

CANRH

ROFEY

PEHANP

COSLIA

You don't have any trumpets?

No. We don't sell those here.

THE TRUMPETER COULDN'T FIND A REPLACEMENT TRUMPET IN PARIS BECAUSE THEY ONLY SOLD ---

Now arrange the circled letters to form the surprise answer, as suggested by the above cartoon.

Print answer here

JUMBLE®

Unscramble these four Jumbles, one letter to
each square, to form four ordinary words.

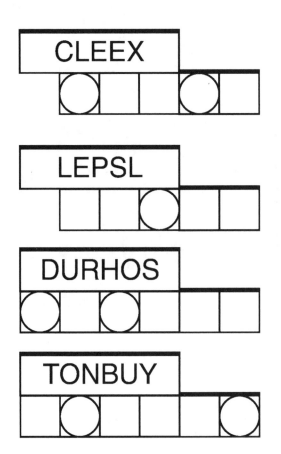

CLEEX

LEPSL

DURHOS

TONBUY

Howdy, neighbors!

Look at that mess! How can he live like that?

People say I'm messy.

WHEN THE CYCLOPS MOVED
INTO THE NEIGHBORHOOD,
HIS MESSY YARD WAS AN ----

Now arrange the circled letters to form
the surprise answer, as suggested by the
above cartoon.

Print answer here

JUMBLE®

Unscramble these four Jumbles, one letter to
each square, to form four ordinary words.

SOTHI

YOEMN

LATNEY

DIRSAH

I'm placing you
under arrest.
Now, I'm going to
read you your
rights. Pay close
attention.

WHEN HE WAS
ARRESTED, THE MIME
CHOSE TO ----

Now arrange the circled letters to form
the surprise answer, as suggested by the
above cartoon.

Print
answer
here

JUMBLE®

Unscramble these four Jumbles, one letter to each square, to form four ordinary words.

NALTP

TAGOL

SURIDA

RUTFOH

Hey! The truth hurts! That's it. I'm done with you.

I can't believe you said that!

THEY PARACHUTED TOGETHER ON A REGULAR BASIS UNTIL THEY HAD A ---

Now arrange the circled letters to form the surprise answer, as suggested by the above cartoon.

Print answer here

JUMBLE®

Unscramble these four Jumbles, one letter to each square, to form four ordinary words.

DUBYD

FREAT

PIPTUL

XESESC

Yes! Best job ever!

Per your contract, we'll pay you nine months full pay.

HE WAS THIS AFTER HEARING THE DETAILS OF HIS JOB SEVERANCE PACKAGE ----

Now arrange the circled letters to form the surprise answer, as suggested by the above cartoon.

Print answer here

JUMBLE®

Unscramble these four Jumbles, one letter to each square, to form four ordinary words.

YAWER

LUDBI

GNEELT

YEMNEZ

Those look great!

You can't beat the price.

Buy One Pair, Get One Free.

THEY BOUGHT THE DISCOUNTED SUNGLASSES AFTER SEEING THAT THEY WERE ----

Now arrange the circled letters to form the surprise answer, as suggested by the above cartoon.

Print answer here " ☐☐☐ - ☐☐☐☐ "

JUMBLE®

Unscramble these four Jumbles, one letter to each square, to form four ordinary words.

SEYZT

ATUBO

WORYDS

CLYHIR

The ink purchase is mine. The new laptop is also mine. But I don't have a clue about the Hobbit DVDs.

J.K. ROWLING NOTICED SOME CHARGES ON HER CREDIT CARD BILL THAT WEREN'T ———

Now arrange the circled letters to form the surprise answer, as suggested by the above cartoon.

Print answer here "◯◯◯◯◯◯ - ◯◯◯◯"

MONSTER JUMBLE®

Daily Puzzles

JUMBLE®

Unscramble these four Jumbles, one letter to
each square, to form four ordinary words.

CANIB

BARRO

FAMALE

TACILI

ARRIVALS
DEPARTURES

We can get you on the
earlier flight for $600.
Would you like a
middle seat? Do you
have luggage?

What! My
ticket only
cost $300!
You have
plenty of
seats!

THE COST TO CHANGE HIS
FLIGHT WAS GOING TO BE
$600. HE DIDN'T THINK
THAT WAS ----

Now arrange the circled letters to form
the surprise answer, as suggested by the
above cartoon.

Print answer here " ◯◯◯ - ◯◯◯◯ "

28

JUMBLE®

Unscramble these four Jumbles, one letter to each square, to form four ordinary words.

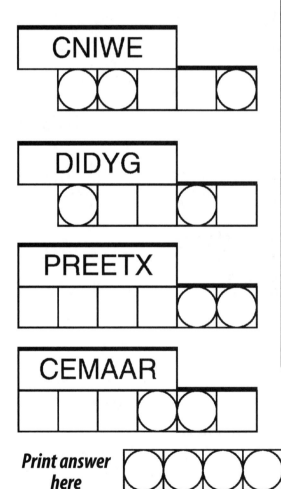

CNIWE

DIDYG

PREETX

CEMAAR

Wow! You've been busy today. Are you going to come inside soon?

I still have more to do and the energy to keep going.

SHE PLANNED TO WORK IN HER GARDEN UNTIL SHE ----

Now arrange the circled letters to form the surprise answer, as suggested by the above cartoon.

Print answer here

29

JUMBLE®

Unscramble these four Jumbles, one letter to each square, to form four ordinary words.

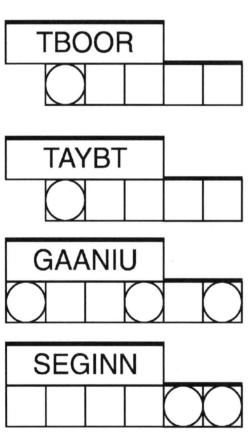

TBOOR

TAYBT

GAANIU

SEGINN

Excellent. Acquiring your drinking establishment for a cash discount makes this deal better for me.

I can really use the money.

MOE'S

FOR SALE

HE BOUGHT THE TAVERN BECAUSE IT WAS A ---

Now arrange the circled letters to form the surprise answer, as suggested by the above cartoon.

Print answer here

30

JUMBLE

Unscramble these four Jumbles, one letter to
each square, to form four ordinary words.

PADTA

LMAPC

SPRIMH

FLYDON

Are you coming to the conference room?

Nope. I have to get the Hoyt project to city hall for approval.

THE ARCHITECT COULDN'T
STAY FOR THE MEETING
BECAUSE HE ----

Now arrange the circled letters to form
the surprise answer, as suggested by the
above cartoon.

Print answer here

31

JUMBLE®

Unscramble these four Jumbles, one letter to each square, to form four ordinary words.

DURPO

YHLSY

ROBHET

RATSAY

DOMINICK'S

Are you stopping for a drink?

Come on! It's happy hour. You can study later.

Not tonight. I need to study.

HAPPY HOUR 4-8

THE LAW STUDENT DECLINED GOING TO THE TAVERN SO HE COULD ----

Now arrange the circled letters to form the surprise answer, as suggested by the above cartoon.

Print answer here

JUMBLE®

Unscramble these four Jumbles, one letter to each square, to form four ordinary words.

SLOPI

PUROG

DENMAT

CITANT

ADVERTISE HERE!

We can give you the first three months for free.

Everyone can see it here. I'm in!

WHEN THEY OFFERED HER A CHANCE TO ADVERTISE ON THE BILLBOARD AT A DISCOUNT, SHE SAID ----

Now arrange the circled letters to form the surprise answer, as suggested by the above cartoon.

Print answer here

33

JUMBLE®

Unscramble these four Jumbles, one letter to each square, to form four ordinary words.

UGEGO

OSEHU

TENXET

NACDEN

I love coming here.

I'm here all the time.

THE BAT BAR WAS BECOMING A POPULAR ---

Now arrange the circled letters to form the surprise answer, as suggested by the above cartoon.

Print answer here

34

JUMBLE®

Unscramble these four Jumbles, one letter to each square, to form four ordinary words.

PENIT

TOCUS

MAGLEB

DEHLUD

THE FUNERAL HOME DIRECTOR READ HIS BOOK IN ---

Now arrange the circled letters to form the surprise answer, as suggested by the above cartoon.

Print answer here

35

JUMBLE®

Unscramble these four Jumbles, one letter to each square, to form four ordinary words.

NACPI

DEYSE

GEETRR

GOOLNB

Thanks for coming in from Sydney.

Anything for friends.

He's pretty good.

Best in Australia.

THE ANIMAL BAND NEEDED A NEW DRUMMER, SO THEY HIRED ---

Now arrange the circled letters to form the surprise answer, as suggested by the above cartoon.

Print answer here

36

JUMBLE®

Unscramble these four Jumbles, one letter to each square, to form four ordinary words.

GUNDE

BAITH

DANNIL

OPALHO

Do you remember walking in the park on our first date?

Of course. It was so romantic.

FALLING IN LOVE AND GOING FOR WALKS TOGETHER ---

Now arrange the circled letters to form the surprise answer, as suggested by the above cartoon.

Print answer here

37

JUMBLE®

Unscramble these four Jumbles, one letter to each square, to form four ordinary words.

AKALO

TEENV

SETIFY

DARHIO

My sinuses are all clogged up.

Do you have food allergies?

THE HORSE WASN'T FEELING WELL BECAUSE OF ---

Now arrange the circled letters to form the surprise answer, as suggested by the above cartoon.

Print answer here

JUMBLE®

Unscramble these four Jumbles, one letter to each square, to form four ordinary words.

FINSF

NATGE

DEVIDI

TMOOBT

What are you doing here? You're supposed to be at school. It's Monday!

Huh? I thought it was still the weekend.

SUGAR BOMBS

THE STUDENT FORGOT TO GO TO SCHOOL BECAUSE HE WAS ----

Now arrange the circled letters to form the surprise answer, as suggested by the above cartoon.

Print answer here

$\bigcirc\bigcirc\bigcirc\bigcirc\bigcirc\bigcirc$ - $\bigcirc\bigcirc\bigcirc\bigcirc\bigcirc\bigcirc$

JUMBLE®

Unscramble these four Jumbles, one letter to each square, to form four ordinary words.

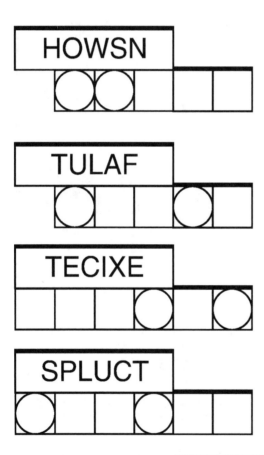

HOWSN

TULAF

TECIXE

SPLUCT

Today's Specials:
Cod 8.99/lb.
Halibut 14.99/lb.
Perch 12.99/lb.

He's never given us a dime more than our wages.

I need these fish sold! I have half a mind to cut your bonus.

What bonus?

THE GREEDY OWNER OF THE SEAFOOD MARKET WAS ---

Now arrange the circled letters to form the surprise answer, as suggested by the above cartoon.

Print answer here " ◯◯◯◯ - ◯◯◯◯ "

JUMBLE®

Unscramble these four Jumbles, one letter to each square, to form four ordinary words.

POHOM

COURC

WULLAF

MANUTU

Here are the next two dresses. Be sure to sparkle.

I'll see what I can do.

AFTER A LONG DAY OF SHOWING OFF THE NEW CLOTHING LINE, THE FASHION MODEL WAS ---

Now arrange the circled letters to form the surprise answer, as suggested by the above cartoon.

Print answer here

41

JUMBLE®

Unscramble these four Jumbles, one letter to each square, to form four ordinary words.

SHULS

BAMUL

RATBYE

FITARD

The smart play is to lay up.

It will take some skill to avoid those bunkers.

TO WIN THE GREEN JACKET AT AUGUSTA, A GOLFER NEEDS TO PLAY ----

Now arrange the circled letters to form the surprise answer, as suggested by the above cartoon.

Print answer here

JUMBLE®

Unscramble these four Jumbles, one letter to each square, to form four ordinary words.

FINTU

DUNOM

TNNITE

KAAILL

I can't believe how tasty this all looks. Just like in my dreams. I must be in heaven.

FRYDAY!

HIS PASSION FOR HIGH-CALORIE FOODS WAS ----

Now arrange the circled letters to form the surprise answer, as suggested by the above cartoon.

Print answer here

43

JUMBLE®

Unscramble these four Jumbles, one letter to each square, to form four ordinary words.

NALST

TUNIP

DUNFOE

GENMAT

That's your property over there.

Oh, no! It was supposed to be farmland.

WHEN THE PIONEERS LEARNED THAT THEIR HOMESTEAD WAS A SWAMP, THE NEWS WAS ----

Now arrange the circled letters to form the surprise answer, as suggested by the above cartoon.

Print answer here

JUMBLE®

Unscramble these four Jumbles, one letter to
each square, to form four ordinary words.

GORRI

ESEGE

ACEVIT

BOLCAT

Here you go!
Do you want it?
You can fetch this
and much more
inside!

You're good
at this.

Good Boy
Canine Sports

THE RETRIEVER'S STORE
WAS SO SUCCESSFUL
BECAUSE HE WAS A ----

Now arrange the circled letters to form
the surprise answer, as suggested by the
above cartoon.

Print
answer
here
⟨⟩⟨⟩⟨⟩⟨⟩ ⟨⟩⟨⟩ - ⟨⟩⟨⟩⟨⟩⟨⟩⟨⟩⟨⟩

45

JUMBLE®

Unscramble these four Jumbles, one letter to
each square, to form four ordinary words.

LIHEW

LIFTN

CUDNIT

DREARH

Do you
have any
idea what
could be
wrong?

Let me play
with it a few
days. I may
need to
adjust the
strings a little.

STRINGS
&
THINGS

HE WASN'T EXACTLY SURE
WHAT WAS WRONG WITH THE
VIOLIN AND NEEDED TO ---

Now arrange the circled letters to form
the surprise answer, as suggested by the
above cartoon.

*Print
answer
here*

46

JUMBLE®

Unscramble these four Jumbles, one letter to each square, to form four ordinary words.

LEYID

SOGBU

COLUNK

GLEEDP

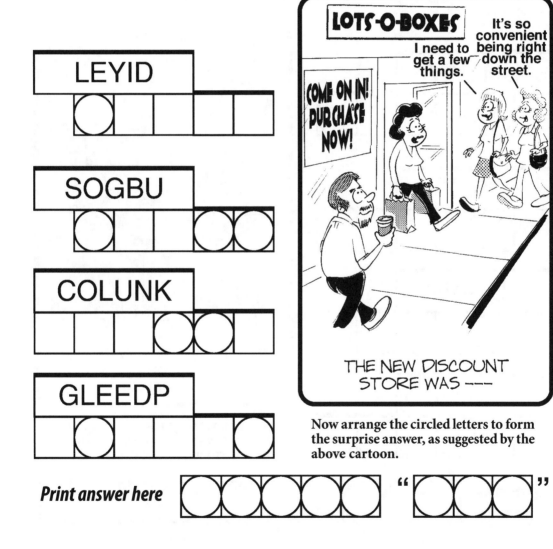

LOTS-O-BOXES

COME ON IN! PURCHASE NOW!

I need to get a few things.

It's so convenient being right down the street.

THE NEW DISCOUNT STORE WAS ----

Now arrange the circled letters to form the surprise answer, as suggested by the above cartoon.

Print answer here ◯◯◯◯◯ " ◯◯◯ "

47

JUMBLE®

Unscramble these four Jumbles, one letter to each square, to form four ordinary words.

CHOAV

PMETT

SUDARI

FEMIDF

Come on, Woody. You need to get some exercise. Go get it! Go get it!

If you wanted me to get it, you should have dropped it.

THE DOG THOUGHT THE IDEA OF RETRIEVING THE BALL WAS ———

Now arrange the circled letters to form the surprise answer, as suggested by the above cartoon.

Print answer here

JUMBLE®

Unscramble these four Jumbles, one letter to each square, to form four ordinary words.

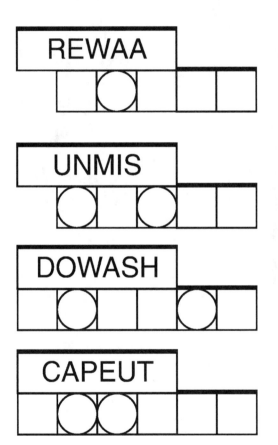

REWAA

UNMIS

DOWASH

CAPEUT

Rusty, just stay here. Don't move.

MEN

THE SIGN ON THE LADIES' ROOM AT THE HORSE RANCH SAID ———

Now arrange the circled letters to form the surprise answer, as suggested by the above cartoon.

Print answer here " ⬡⬡⬡⬡ - ⬡⬡⬡ "

JUMBLE

Unscramble these four Jumbles, one letter to
each square, to form four ordinary words.

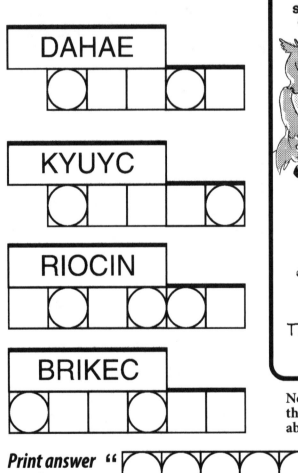

DAHAE

KYUYC

RIOCIN

BRIKEC

What is the world's strongest animal?

The Hercules beetle can lift 850 times its own weight.

Not again.

THE WILD OX DID SO WELL
IN SCHOOL BECAUSE
HE WAS A ----

Now arrange the circled letters to form
the surprise answer, as suggested by the
above cartoon.

Print answer " ⬡⬡⬡⬡⬡⬡⬡ - ⬡⬡⬡ "
here

50

JUMBLE®

Unscramble these four Jumbles, one letter to each square, to form four ordinary words.

KEEVO

DIRGI

AHATYP

EMUDIT

ADOPT A PET TODAY!

I told you, a Toy Poodle will be best for our apartment.

I say this Plott Hound will be great with our kids.

THEY WANTED A PUREBRED DOG WITH A GREAT BLOODLINE, BUT THEY COULDN'T ----

Now arrange the circled letters to form the surprise answer, as suggested by the above cartoon.

Print answer here " ◯◯◯ - ◯◯◯◯◯ "

JUMBLE®

Unscramble these four Jumbles, one letter to each square, to form four ordinary words.

SEDUO

CNARH

PUNOCE

SCEOHO

I like the jobs it's brought.

It's bringing down property values.

THE NEW PRISON HAD ITS ---

Now arrange the circled letters to form the surprise answer, as suggested by the above cartoon.

Print answer here

52

JUMBLE®

Unscramble these four Jumbles, one letter to each square, to form four ordinary words.

PIMLE

CANKK

LEPYUL

TENERL

I'm getting soaked!

The map is ruined.

WHEN THEY GOT CAUGHT IN THE DOWNPOUR IN KIEV, THEY WERE IN THE ----

Now arrange the circled letters to form the surprise answer, as suggested by the above cartoon.

Print answer here " ◯◯ - ◯◯◯◯ - ◯ "

53

JUMBLE®

Unscramble these four Jumbles, one letter to each square, to form four ordinary words.

GOMLU

CLIRE

SHOECN

THILGF

Offsides! Number 72.

You need to relax! Wait until the ball is snapped.

I get excited.

HE WAS CALLED FOR BEING OFFSIDES SO OFTEN BECAUSE HE KEPT ---

Now arrange the circled letters to form the surprise answer, as suggested by the above cartoon.

Print answer here

JUMBLE®

Unscramble these four Jumbles, one letter to each square, to form four ordinary words.

NUGTS

LORLD

NEPCAR

WOATUL

I think it's time I upgrade my phone.

Wow! Shouldn't that be in a museum?

GOOD BUY

TRADING IN HIS OLD CELL PHONE FOR A NEW ONE WAS ----

Now arrange the circled letters to form the surprise answer, as suggested by the above cartoon.

Print answer here A ⬡⬡⬡⬡ ⬡⬡⬡⬡

55

JUMBLE®

Unscramble these four Jumbles, one letter to each square, to form four ordinary words.

LROTL

VIDTO

HITEER

RATAYS

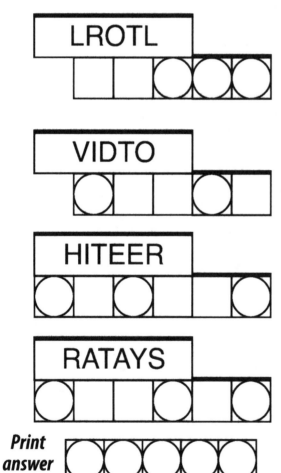

I've got to go. I have league night. I'm going for a new team record tonight.

Stay out of the gutter.

HE HAD HIS BOWLING BALL AND BOWLING SHOES . . . HE WAS ----

Now arrange the circled letters to form the surprise answer, as suggested by the above cartoon.

Print answer here

JUMBLE®

Unscramble these four Jumbles, one letter to each square, to form four ordinary words.

TEYSZ

RAWOR

PONIOS

RICOIN

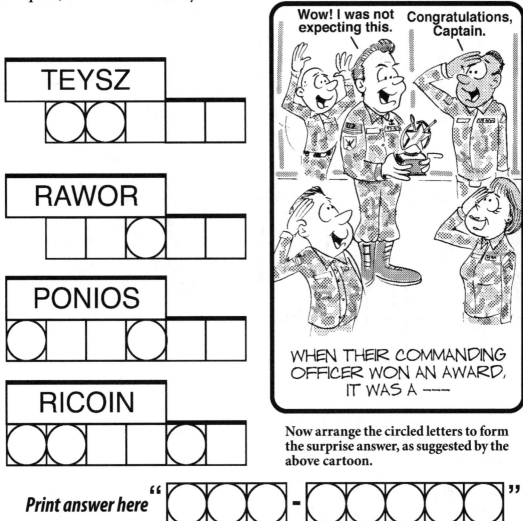

Wow! I was not expecting this.

Congratulations, Captain.

WHEN THEIR COMMANDING OFFICER WON AN AWARD, IT WAS A ---

Now arrange the circled letters to form the surprise answer, as suggested by the above cartoon.

Print answer here "◯◯◯ - ◯◯◯◯◯"

JUMBLE®

Unscramble these four Jumbles, one letter to each square, to form four ordinary words.

TAOFO

ZEDDA

KCTESH

TAMUNU

I'm going to ask her out.

AFTER SEEING HIS NEW CO-WORKER AT THE CALENDAR FACTORY, HE WANTED TO ---

Now arrange the circled letters to form the surprise answer, as suggested by the above cartoon.

Print answer here

JUMBLE®

Unscramble these four Jumbles, one letter to each square, to form four ordinary words.

VAHCO

NABIC

BURNEM

RIDZAL

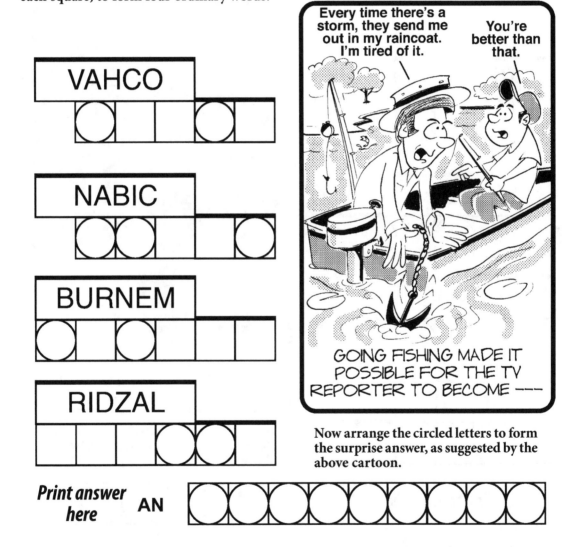

Every time there's a storm, they send me out in my raincoat. I'm tired of it.

You're better than that.

GOING FISHING MADE IT POSSIBLE FOR THE TV REPORTER TO BECOME ———

Now arrange the circled letters to form the surprise answer, as suggested by the above cartoon.

Print answer here   AN ☐☐☐☐☐☐☐☐☐☐

JUMBLE®

Unscramble these four Jumbles, one letter to each square, to form four ordinary words.

VEEAL

STYZE

GEJROG

PAMIGE

Well, that was easy.

He's too big to hide.

WHEN KING KONG ESCAPED FROM CUSTODY, HE WAS ———

Now arrange the circled letters to form the surprise answer, as suggested by the above cartoon.

Print answer here ⬜⬜ ⬜⬜⬜⬜⬜

60

JUMBLE®

Unscramble these four Jumbles, one letter to each square, to form four ordinary words.

WARBN

NOTJI

LADINN

SEMTUK

Can I go to sleep now?

I can't believe I work here! I love sleeping, so this is perfect for me.

TO THE NEW TECHNICIAN, WORKING AT THE SLEEP STUDY INSTITUTE WAS ---

Now arrange the circled letters to form the surprise answer, as suggested by the above cartoon.

Print answer here   A

61

JUMBLE®

Unscramble these four Jumbles, one letter to each square, to form four ordinary words.

UNEVE

CARTT

LODUEM

BIHRDY

You must really love fishing.

This was the only time for us to get out.

I think I've got one!

FISHING WHEN THE WATER WAS LOW WOULD HAVE TO ----

Now arrange the circled letters to form the surprise answer, as suggested by the above cartoon.

Print answer here

62

JUMBLE®

Unscramble these four Jumbles, one letter to each square, to form four ordinary words.

AATIW

DAGEL

DORGUN

DIONGI

Aw, man!

Where are you headed?

THE RUNNER TRIED TO MAKE IT TO THIRD BASE, BUT UNFORTUNATELY FOR HIM, THE SHORTSTOP ----

Now arrange the circled letters to form the surprise answer, as suggested by the above cartoon.

Print answer here

63

JUMBLE®

Unscramble these four Jumbles, one letter to each square, to form four ordinary words.

RIGET

TAMID

DRASTN

ZEPLUZ

This helps me relax.

Nice!

THE CIRCUS PERFORMER PAINTED DURING HIS TIME OFF BECAUSE HE WAS A ---

Now arrange the circled letters to form the surprise answer, as suggested by the above cartoon.

Print answer here

JUMBLE®

Unscramble these four Jumbles, one letter to each square, to form four ordinary words.

UNROD

VEARB

CESKOT

YALXAG

Do we need that much?

They're practically giving it away.

Happy Camper Store

Firewood Buy 1 Get 1 FREE!

THE SALE ON THE FIREWOOD ALLOWED THE CAMPER TO ---

Now arrange the circled letters to form the surprise answer, as suggested by the above cartoon.

Print answer here

65

JUMBLE

Unscramble these four Jumbles, one letter to each square, to form four ordinary words.

DOMEM

WRAPN

LOGNAL

KIOROE

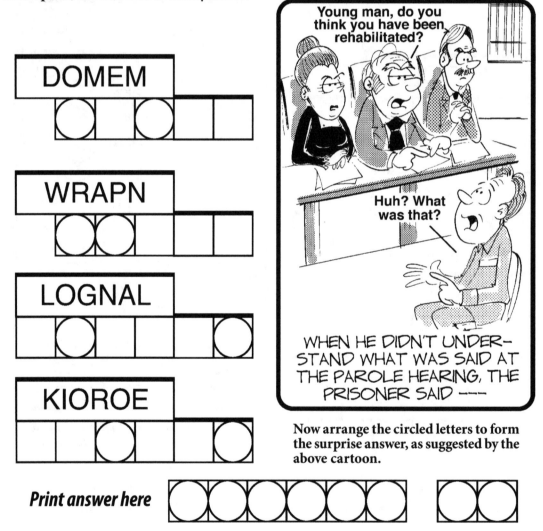

Young man, do you think you have been rehabilitated?

Huh? What was that?

WHEN HE DIDN'T UNDER-STAND WHAT WAS SAID AT THE PAROLE HEARING, THE PRISONER SAID ---

Now arrange the circled letters to form the surprise answer, as suggested by the above cartoon.

Print answer here

66

JUMBLE®

Unscramble these four Jumbles, one letter to each square, to form four ordinary words.

RUNPS

CROPH

CHATED

SIORRE

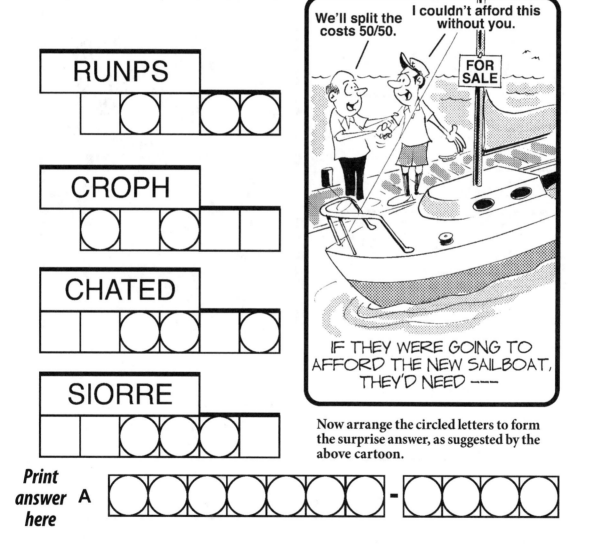

We'll split the costs 50/50.

I couldn't afford this without you.

FOR SALE

IF THEY WERE GOING TO AFFORD THE NEW SAILBOAT, THEY'D NEED ----

Now arrange the circled letters to form the surprise answer, as suggested by the above cartoon.

Print answer here   A ⬡⬡⬡⬡⬡⬡⬡ - ⬡⬡⬡⬡

JUMBLE®

Unscramble these four Jumbles, one letter to each square, to form four ordinary words.

GURYB

DOIVE

BUSTIM

TORTEA

JUMBLE Outlet Store
BUY IMMEDIATELY!
PURCHASE NOW!
ACT QUICKLY!
2 miles ahead Exit 404

We should stop there.

I ♥ JUMBL

THE BILLBOARD FEATURED ---

Now arrange the circled letters to form the surprise answer, as suggested by the above cartoon.

Print answer here

JUMBLE®

Unscramble these four Jumbles, one letter to each square, to form four ordinary words.

PIRGE

RUMON

TOBMOT

AKENEW

You know, if you got a job, you'd be able to afford to leave the house once in awhile.

No, thanks. I'm good.

HER ATTEMPT TO MAKE HER TEENAGE SON GET A PART-TIME JOB WAS ---

Now arrange the circled letters to form the surprise answer, as suggested by the above cartoon.

Print answer here

69

JUMBLE®

Unscramble these four Jumbles, one letter to each square, to form four ordinary words.

NARCK

THIET

ROSELC

SAYDIM

This can't be right. I should have made more.

After taxes, that's what you get.

YUM!

THE NEW EMPLOYEE WAS UNHAPPY ON HIS FIRST PAYDAY BECAUSE HE GOT A ----

Now arrange the circled letters to form the surprise answer, as suggested by the above cartoon.

Print answer here

A

JUMBLE®

Unscramble these four Jumbles, one letter to each square, to form four ordinary words.

PARCM

NOORM

WONDAR

TUDNIP

Oh my gosh! Why's everybody kung fu fighting?

Kingdom: Animalia
Phylum: Chordata
Class: Mammalia
Order: Carnivora
Family: Ursidae
Genus: Ailuropoda
Species: A. melanoleuca

WHAT THE ZOOKEEPER WITNESSED IN THE ASIAN ANIMAL SECTION.

Now arrange the circled letters to form the surprise answer, as suggested by the above cartoon.

Print answer here

" ◯◯◯◯◯ - ◯◯◯◯◯◯ "

JUMBLE®

Unscramble these four Jumbles, one letter to each square, to form four ordinary words.

LIGUT

LEHEW

PECROP

STORYF

Uh-oh.

Noooo! I can't believe this!

WHEN HER PRICELESS MING VASE CRASHED TO THE FLOOR, SHE ----

Now arrange the circled letters to form the surprise answer, as suggested by the above cartoon.

Print answer here

72

JUMBLE®

Unscramble these four Jumbles, one letter to
each square, to form four ordinary words.

NEMOY

FRASC

TORPIF

YAGELL

I think the butler
should be the killer.

Too predictable.
I think the cop
should be the
killer.

THE SCREENWRITERS DIDN'T
WORK WELL TOGETHER
BECAUSE THEY COULDN'T
GET ---

Now arrange the circled letters to form
the surprise answer, as suggested by the
above cartoon.

Print
answer
here

THE

73

JUMBLE®

Unscramble these four Jumbles, one letter to each square, to form four ordinary words.

TOLUC

CREPH

CADORC

LEBFEE

White
Green
Black
Earl Grey

Yuk!
I didn't order
cappuccino!

SHE DIDN'T LIKE
THE COFFEE BECAUSE IT
WASN'T THIS.

Now arrange the circled letters to form the surprise answer, as suggested by the above cartoon.

Print answer here

JUMBLE®

Unscramble these four Jumbles, one letter to each square, to form four ordinary words.

RHOON

LUTAF

LAGNOL

GRYNUH

This looks good. Let us proceed.

I will have it printed up for tomorrow.

ON JULY 3, 1776, THE FOUNDING FATHERS DECIDED THAT THEY SHOULD ---

Now arrange the circled letters to form the surprise answer, as suggested by the above cartoon.

Print answer here ⬡⬡ " ⬡⬡⬡⬡⬡⬡ "

75

JUMBLE®

Unscramble these four Jumbles, one letter to each square, to form four ordinary words.

DOWUN

FUTIN

TODEEN

ROARAU

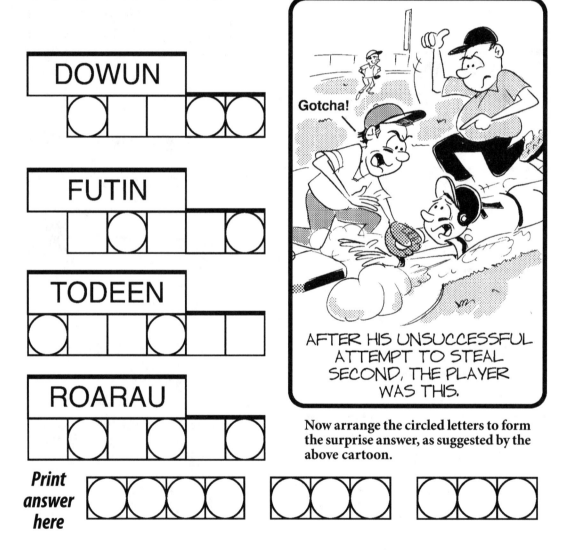

Gotcha!

AFTER HIS UNSUCCESSFUL ATTEMPT TO STEAL SECOND, THE PLAYER WAS THIS.

Now arrange the circled letters to form the surprise answer, as suggested by the above cartoon.

Print answer here

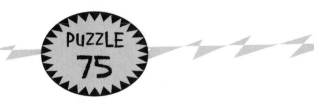

JUMBLE®

Unscramble these four Jumbles, one letter to each square, to form four ordinary words.

SOGOE

CIXTO

TUNTAR

SCAWEH

Let's not get rid of him yet. There's still time for him to recover.

THE PERFORMER STRUGGLED UNTIL HE GOT HIS ---

Now arrange the circled letters to form the surprise answer, as suggested by the above cartoon.

Print answer here

JUMBLE®

Unscramble these four Jumbles, one letter to each square, to form four ordinary words.

TOBOH

TOLCH

WEVELT

ADDNEW

I've given this a lot of thought...I won't be running for president.

No one was going to vote for him anyway.

Jeff ★★ 2012

HE WAS GOING TO RUN FOR PRESIDENT, BUT IN THE END HE ----

Now arrange the circled letters to form the surprise answer, as suggested by the above cartoon.

Print answer here

78

JUMBLE®

Unscramble these four Jumbles, one letter to
each square, to form four ordinary words.

All done!
Let's celebrate.

The city
awaits.

TOMHN

ETONK

LAWPOL

SPITYG

AFTER FINALLY FINISHING
THE MURAL, THE ARTIST
WANTED TO DO THIS.

Now arrange the circled letters to form
the surprise answer, as suggested by the
above cartoon.

Print
answer
here

JUMBLE®

Unscramble these four Jumbles, one letter to each square, to form four ordinary words.

NIHYS

AWERF

CLUNKO

UNBEOC

Everything looks great. I'll see you next time.

That's it? We're done?

HER VISIT TO THE EYE DOCTOR WAS OVER IN THE ---

Now arrange the circled letters to form the surprise answer, as suggested by the above cartoon.

Print answer here

JUMBLE®

Unscramble these four Jumbles, one letter to each square, to form four ordinary words.

DIGRI

DOVIA

GTREER

TACELT

I think I'm ready. I'm going to attempt to compete.

AFTER HE TRAINED BY RUNNING, CYCLING AND SWIMMING, THE ATHLETE DECIDED TO ---

Now arrange the circled letters to form the surprise answer, as suggested by the above cartoon.

Print answer here   "   "

JUMBLE®

Unscramble these four Jumbles, one letter to each square, to form four ordinary words.

SMEYS

HAFRW

DIHNED

CESBIP

I'll be back for the next group soon.

EVERGLADE BOB

HE WAS THIS AS A RESULT OF HIS BOOMING AIRBOAT BUSINESS.

Now arrange the circled letters to form the surprise answer, as suggested by the above cartoon.

Print answer here

JUMBLE®

Unscramble these four Jumbles, one letter to each square, to form four ordinary words.

BAINC

NARBD

TABMIG

GEBBUD

WHAT WERE THEY PLAYING AT THE PURSE COUNTER?

Now arrange the circled letters to form the surprise answer, as suggested by the above cartoon.

Print answer here

83

JUMBLE®

Unscramble these four Jumbles, one letter to each square, to form four ordinary words. —

TOUHY

HEMIC

TEABED

YENTIC

Oops!

I see you made it

HOW SHE ARRIVED AT HER DESTINATION.

Now arrange the circled letters to form the surprise answer, as suggested by the above cartoon.

Print answer here

84

JUMBLE®

Unscramble these four Jumbles, one letter to each square, to form four ordinary words.

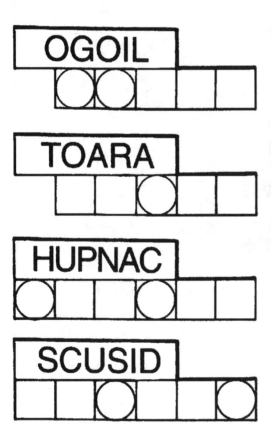

OGOIL

TOARA

HUPNAC

SCUSID

CAR RENTAL AGENCY

THEY CONTRACT TO GIVE YOU A COMFORTABLE RIDE.

Now arrange the circled letters to form the surprise answer, as suggested by the above cartoon.

Print answer here

JUMBLE®

Unscramble these four Jumbles, one letter to each square, to form four ordinary words.

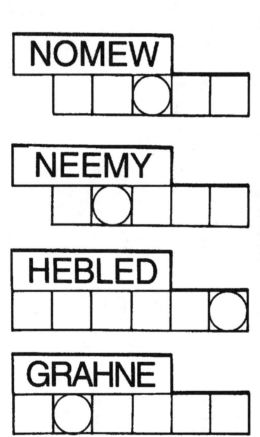

NOMEW

NEEMY

HEBLED

GRAHNE

Ready for surgery

WHAT A DOCTOR PUTS ON BEFORE HE STARTS WORKING.

Now arrange the circled letters to form the surprise answer, as suggested by the above cartoon.

Print answer here

86

JUMBLE®

Unscramble these four Jumbles, one letter to each square, to form four ordinary words.

FEBIT

COVAL

RAMPUK

RYTHOF

SILVERWARE

WHAT THEY SAID WHEN THEY HELD UP THE SHOP.

Now arrange the circled letters to form the surprise answer, as suggested by the above cartoon.

Print answer here

JUMBLE®

Unscramble these four Jumbles, one letter to each square, to form four ordinary words.

LYKIM

REVUC

SNUFUG

BASURD

THIS CALLS FOR THE ARMY!

Now arrange the circled letters to form the surprise answer, as suggested by the above cartoon.

Print answer here

88

JUMBLE®

Unscramble these four Jumbles, one letter to each square, to form four ordinary words.

SYNIH

GUCOH

ENCOSH

TAUBEY

WHAT THE TEAM DIDN'T HAVE WHEN IT LOST ITS "SPIRIT."

Now arrange the circled letters to form the surprise answer, as suggested by the above cartoon.

Print answer here A ⬜⬜⬜⬜⬜ OF A ⬜⬜⬜⬜⬜⬜

JUMBLE®

Unscramble these four Jumbles, one letter to each square, to form four ordinary words.

YUINF

SUGIE

DEECES

CRASAF

Busybody!

THOSE WHO TAKE IT ARE OUT FOR THE COUNT.

Now arrange the circled letters to form the surprise answer, as suggested by the above cartoon.

Print answer here

JUMBLE ®

Unscramble these four Jumbles, one letter to each square, to form four ordinary words.

HIWGE

SCUFO

STEPEL

FLAINE

Vote for me and your government will take care of you

PEOPLE WOULD EXPECT THEIR SUPPORT FROM CRADLE TO GRAVE.

Now arrange the circled letters to form the surprise answer, as suggested by the above cartoon.

Print answer here

91

JUMBLE®

Unscramble these four Jumbles, one letter to
each square, to form four ordinary words.

PLITO

NITLE

FREBLY

GLOANS

Yes, guv'nor

'E's just
received
a knight-
hood

WHAT THEY CALLED
THE BRITISH
BEEF TYCOON.

Now arrange the circled letters to form
the surprise answer, as suggested by the
above cartoon.

Print answer here " ◯◯◯ ◯◯◯◯ "

JUMBLE®

Unscramble these four Jumbles, one letter to each square, to form four ordinary words.

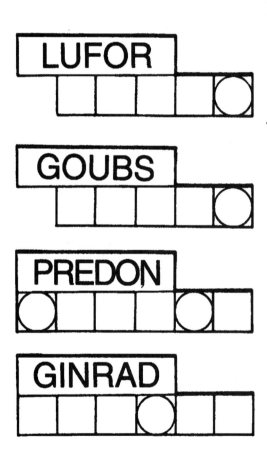

LUFOR

GOUBS

PREDON

GINRAD

THEY OFTEN GO OUT TO SEA IN PORTS.

Now arrange the circled letters to form the surprise answer, as suggested by the above cartoon.

Print answer here ⬡⬡⬡⬡⬡

93

JUMBLE®

Unscramble these four Jumbles, one letter to each square, to form four ordinary words.

MARDA

ASTUE

CAFEDE

MUBHEL

Means a lot of hard work

HE SAID THIS WAS THE ACTING GAME.

Now arrange the circled letters to form the surprise answer, as suggested by the above cartoon.

Print answer here

JUMBLE®

Unscramble these four Jumbles, one letter to each square, to form four ordinary words.

SEECA

SYNAP

INLOOT

LUBOSE

TAKE IN HAND FOR A BATH!

Now arrange the circled letters to form the surprise answer, as suggested by the above cartoon.

Print answer here

95

JUMBLE®

Unscramble these four Jumbles, one letter to
each square, to form four ordinary words.

ICMEN

GEDEH

VODURE

TENAGE

— Let's split!

A KIND OF
SURREPTITIOUS
BALL PLAYING.

Now arrange the circled letters to form
the surprise answer, as suggested by the
above cartoon.

Print answer here "◯◯◯◯◯◯◯◯◯◯"

96

JUMBLE®

Unscramble these four Jumbles, one letter to each square, to form four ordinary words.

NUCOE

MYNAL

DOSTIL

SYMICT

What's it mean?

Check the dictionary

IN A WORD, IT MEANS THE SAME THING!

Now arrange the circled letters to form the surprise answer, as suggested by the above cartoon.

Print answer here

JUMBLE®

Unscramble these four Jumbles, one letter to each square, to form four ordinary words.

ROHAB

ISTOC

MYSILF

TANIED

Who's playing the lead?

THE BEST PART OF THE THEATER.

Now arrange the circled letters to form the surprise answer, as suggested by the above cartoon.

Print answer here □□□ □□□□'□

98

JUMBLE®

Unscramble these four Jumbles, one letter to each square, to form four ordinary words.

LANUN

NIORB

TARIPE

TIMOON

MEN IN PORT ARE CONSPICUOUS.

Now arrange the circled letters to form the surprise answer, as suggested by the above cartoon.

Print answer here

JUMBLE®

Unscramble these four Jumbles, one letter to
each square, to form four ordinary words.

MIDIO

PRUNS

REEFIC

HARTOU

THE BACK PART
OF THESE
WEAPONS IS IN
THE CENTER.

Now arrange the circled letters to form
the surprise answer, as suggested by the
above cartoon.

Print answer here " ◯◯ - ◯◯◯◯◯ - ◯◯ "

100

JUMBLE®

Unscramble these four Jumbles, one letter to each square, to form four ordinary words.

STACE

KAFLE

THROYP

ROOVED

IT'S AGAINST THE LAW TO PICK THEM IN PARKS.

Now arrange the circled letters to form the surprise answer, as suggested by the above cartoon.

Print answer here

101

JUMBLE®

Unscramble these four Jumbles, one letter to each square, to form four ordinary words.

MEERY

DISTA

SKENIC

TIXECE

MAY DISCOVER A NEW STAR.

Now arrange the circled letters to form the surprise answer, as suggested by the above cartoon.

Print answer here   A

JUMBLE®

Unscramble these four Jumbles, one letter to each square, to form four ordinary words.

TIBUL

HUMOT

ALESEW

DIRAUM

WHAT KIND OF WAITER WON'T ACCEPT A TIP?

Now arrange the circled letters to form the surprise answer, as suggested by the above cartoon.

Print answer here A ◯◯◯◯◯ ◯◯◯◯◯◯◯

103

JUMBLE®

Unscramble these four Jumbles, one letter to
each square, to form four ordinary words.

HARNC

ACTUD

GOYAVE

MAGITS

THE KIND OF TIME
SHE HAD SHOPPING
FOR A DRESS.

Now arrange the circled letters to form
the surprise answer, as suggested by the
above cartoon.

Print answer here "

JUMBLE®

Unscramble these four Jumbles, one letter to each square, to form four ordinary words.

THYIC

FOTOA

TOYBAN

MOFTEN

WHAT THE FOURTH OFFENDER DRUNK HAD TO BE WARY OF.

Now arrange the circled letters to form the surprise answer, as suggested by the above cartoon.

Print answer here

105

JUMBLE®

Unscramble these four Jumbles, one letter to each square, to form four ordinary words.

FELCT

PLEEX

FULOWE

HORDIA

HOW THE COBBLER HOPED TO LEAVE HIS FAMILY.

Now arrange the circled letters to form the surprise answer, as suggested by the above cartoon.

Print answer here ◯◯◯◯ – ◯◯◯◯◯◯

JUMBLE®

Unscramble these four Jumbles, one letter to each square, to form four ordinary words.

JECET

CLUNE

ORFALL

ACCUST

WHAT THE NEWLY-MARRIED SALAD KING BEGGED THE PRESS TO DO.

Now arrange the circled letters to form the surprise answer, as suggested by the above cartoon.

Print answer here " ⬡⬡⬡⬡⬡⬡⬡ " ⬡⬡⬡⬡⬡

107

JUMBLE®

Unscramble these four Jumbles, one letter to
each square, to form four ordinary words.

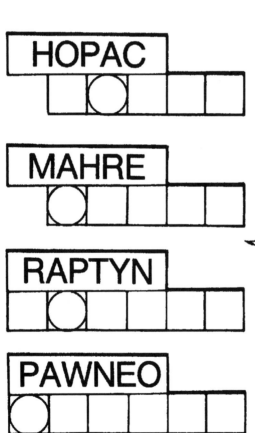

HOPAC

MAHRE

RAPTYN

PAWNEO

WHAT LADY GODIVA
SAID AT THE END
OF HER RIDE.

Now arrange the circled letters to form
the surprise answer, as suggested by the
above cartoon.

Print answer here " ⃝⃝⃝⃝ "

108

JUMBLE®

Unscramble these four Jumbles, one letter to
each square, to form four ordinary words.

LASIA

GINIC

CAGNEY

LAYDED

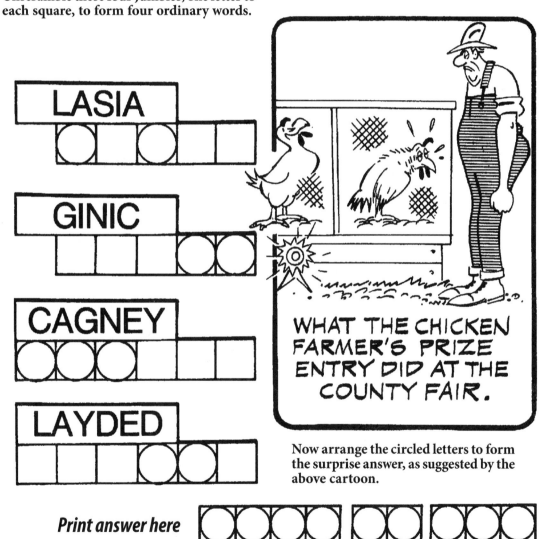

WHAT THE CHICKEN
FARMER'S PRIZE
ENTRY DID AT THE
COUNTY FAIR.

Now arrange the circled letters to form
the surprise answer, as suggested by the
above cartoon.

Print answer here

JUMBLE®

Unscramble these four Jumbles, one letter to each square, to form four ordinary words.

TURBS

BEPOR

KORSEM

SAUTLE

WHAT DID THEY CALL THE CAT THAT FELL INTO THE PICKLE BARREL?

Now arrange the circled letters to form the surprise answer, as suggested by the above cartoon.

Print answer here   A " ⬡⬡⬡⬡ ⬡⬡⬡⬡ "

110

JUMBLE®

Unscramble these four Jumbles, one letter to each square, to form four ordinary words.

HUTEC

LOXET

NECCIS

CREBIK

We've all been friends for so long

THE LADIES IN THE SEWING CIRCLE WERE---

Now arrange the circled letters to form the surprise answer, as suggested by the above cartoon.

Print answer here

111

JUMBLE®

Unscramble these four Jumbles, one letter to
each square, to form four ordinary words.

RIMEN

HAFES

DOHOKE

BOLUDE

Great head for business

SOMETHING LARGELY
RESPONSIBLE FOR
THE PASTA KING'S
SUCCESS.

Now arrange the circled letters to form
the surprise answer, as suggested by the
above cartoon.

Print answer here

112

JUMBLE®

Unscramble these four Jumbles, one letter to each square, to form four ordinary words.

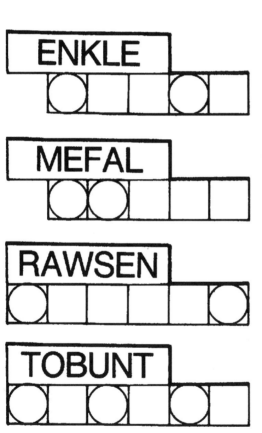

ENKLE

MEFAL

RAWSEN

TOBUNT

YOU MIGHT BE THIS WHEN YOUR APARTMENT COSTS MORE THAN YOU CAN AFFORD.

Now arrange the circled letters to form the surprise answer, as suggested by the above cartoon.

Print answer here

113

JUMBLE®

Unscramble these four Jumbles, one letter to each square, to form four ordinary words.

TUXEL

TAGOL

HECARB

FATOLA

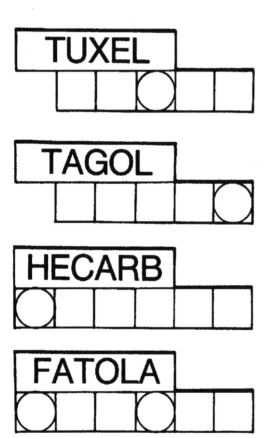

I want you both to come out and kill each other

WHAT THE BOXER WAS WORRIED ABOUT.

Now arrange the circled letters to form the surprise answer, as suggested by the above cartoon.

Print answer here

114

JUMBLE®

Unscramble these four Jumbles, one letter to
each square, to form four ordinary words.

TIPEY

KEVOE

MAROFT

SOPHIL

WHAT SOME
PEOPLE WHO RUN
FOR OFFICES
PROBABLY DID.

Now arrange the circled letters to form
the surprise answer, as suggested by the
above cartoon.

Print answer here

JUMBLE®

Unscramble these four Jumbles, one letter to each square, to form four ordinary words.

DRAYT

SUDOE

GUBORE

MORTER

WHAT DUNKING MIGHT BE, BESIDES BEING BAD MANNERS.

Now arrange the circled letters to form the surprise answer, as suggested by the above cartoon.

Print answer here

JUMBLE®

Unscramble these four Jumbles, one letter to each square, to form four ordinary words.

AMMIX

NIDEK

TRAISE

VEEDIC

WHAT THE TERRIBLE-TEMPERED SUGAR GROWER DID.

Now arrange the circled letters to form the surprise answer, as suggested by the above cartoon.

Print answer here

JUMBLE®

Unscramble these four Jumbles, one letter to
each square, to form four ordinary words.

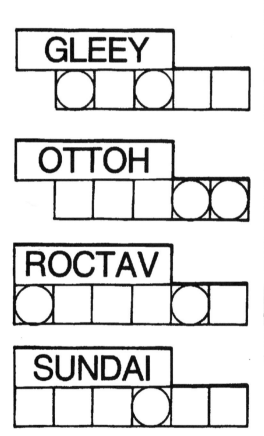

GLEEY

OTTOH

ROCTAV

SUNDAI

Wow! 100%
in math!

Extra
credit
for
neatness

A PERSON WHO
MAKES LITTLE
THINGS COUNT.

Now arrange the circled letters to form
the surprise answer, as suggested by the
above cartoon.

Print answer here A

JUMBLE®

Unscramble these four Jumbles, one letter to each square, to form four ordinary words.

DESET

TRAIE

NERUNG

WARMOR

Hey — wanna get killed?!

SCREECH!

WHAT JAYWALKERS MAY BE WEARING TOMORROW.

Now arrange the circled letters to form the surprise answer, as suggested by the above cartoon.

Print answer here ◯◯◯◯◯

119

JUMBLE®

Unscramble these four Jumbles, one letter to
each square, to form four ordinary words.

GNAAP

YWDDO

CEDBEK

WURFOR

That does it!!

WHAT A FEW
CATTY REMARKS
TURNED THE LADIES'
LOUNGE INTO.

Now arrange the circled letters to form
the surprise answer, as suggested by the
above cartoon.

Print answer here A ◯◯◯◯◯◯ ◯◯◯

JUMBLE

Unscramble these four Jumbles, one letter to each square, to form four ordinary words.

CONIT

VOLEN

ZERBAL

REFTER

THE MANAGER SAID THE PINCH HITTER WOULD BE A CHANGE ---

Now arrange the circled letters to form the surprise answer, as suggested by the above cartoon.

Print answer here ⬡⬡⬡ THE "⬡⬡⬡⬡⬡⬡"

121

JUMBLE®

Unscramble these four Jumbles, one letter to
each square, to form four ordinary words.

NATEC

YUCIJ

CORCUN

POITTE

WHAT A PICNIC
WITH KIDS
SOMETIMES IS.

Now arrange the circled letters to form
the surprise answer, as suggested by the
above cartoon.

Print answer here "◯◯ ◯◯◯◯◯◯◯"

122

JUMBLE®

Unscramble these four Jumbles, one letter to each square, to form four ordinary words.

POUMI

RINPT

AVGASE

MARPHE

Yes, I knew we'd be in agreement

WHEN SHE WANTS HER HUSBAND'S OPINION---

Now arrange the circled letters to form the surprise answer, as suggested by the above cartoon.

Print answer here SHE ⬡⬡⬡⬡⬡ IT ⬡⬡ ⬡⬡⬡

JUMBLE

Unscramble these four Jumbles, one letter to each square, to form four ordinary words.

THABE

YUHRR

DELPOW

RANCAL

WHERE THE HEAVY-WEIGHT CHAMPIONSHIP WAS HELD.

Now arrange the circled letters to form the surprise answer, as suggested by the above cartoon.

Print answer here AT THE " _____ _____ "

124

JUMBLE

Unscramble these four Jumbles, one letter to each square, to form four ordinary words.

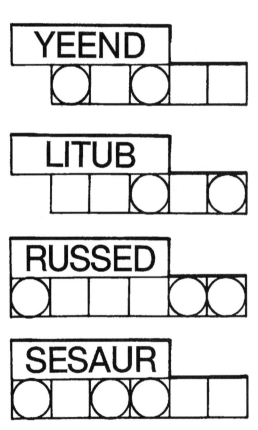

YEEND

LITUB

RUSSED

SESAUR

Egotist!

HE WAS CARRYING ON A GREAT LOVE AFFAIR ---

Now arrange the circled letters to form the surprise answer, as suggested by the above cartoon.

Print answer here

125

JUMBLE®

Unscramble these four Jumbles, one letter to each square, to form four ordinary words.

GOSUB

MOROG

RAYPER

MORRET

WHAT THE FORMER BODYBUILDER'S TORSO BECAME AS HE REACHED MIDDLE AGE.

Now arrange the circled letters to form the surprise answer, as suggested by the above cartoon.

Print answer here

JUMBLE®

Unscramble these four Jumbles, one letter to each square, to form four ordinary words.

DEHIC

SABSY

FLIECK

REPUPA

I'll show 'em

HE DIDN'T BELIEVE IN BEING SUPERSTITIOUS BECAUSE HE THOUGHT IT MIGHT BRING HIM THIS.

Now arrange the circled letters to form the surprise answer, as suggested by the above cartoon.

Print answer here

JUMBLE®

Unscramble these four Jumbles, one letter to each square, to form four ordinary words.

CEHEN

OVEBA

UMLOVE

PATELA

WHAT SHE SAID TO HER BOYFRIEND.

Now arrange the circled letters to form the surprise answer, as suggested by the above cartoon.

Print answer here   YOU "⬡⬡⬡⬡" ⬡⬡⬡⬡⬡⬡⬡

128

JUMBLE®

Unscramble these four Jumbles, one letter to each square, to form four ordinary words.

GLAVE

ILVIC

RANLYX

ACTUFE

We'll be pooped tomorrow   Who cares?

SOME PEOPLE WHO GO "ALL OUT" OFTEN END UP ---

Now arrange the circled letters to form the surprise answer, as suggested by the above cartoon.

Print answer here " ☐☐☐ ☐☐ "

129

JUMBLE®

Unscramble these four Jumbles, one letter to
each square, to form four ordinary words.

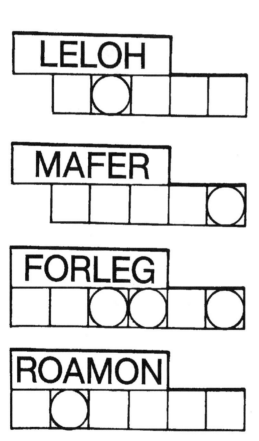

LELOH

MAFER

FORLEG

ROAMON

WHAT THE ARRIVAL
OF SPRING AFTER
A MISERABLE WINTER
SHOULD BRING.

Now arrange the circled letters to form
the surprise answer, as suggested by the
above cartoon.

Print answer here " ⬭⬭ – ⬭⬭⬭⬭ "

JUMBLE®

Unscramble these four Jumbles, one letter to each square, to form four ordinary words.

SWEYN

OSOGE

DEECES

BEHREY

Watch what you say in this crowd

WHAT IT TAKES TO "BRIDLE" ONE'S TONGUE.

Now arrange the circled letters to form the surprise answer, as suggested by the above cartoon.

Print answer here

131

JUMBLE®

Unscramble these four Jumbles, one letter to each square, to form four ordinary words.

TACUE

KROOB

NUPWOT

ENKASH

STRIKE THREE!

You don't look well

HOW THE BALL-PLAYER FELT ON AN OFF DAY.

Now arrange the circled letters to form the surprise answer, as suggested by the above cartoon.

Print answer here ◯◯◯ OF " ◯◯◯◯◯ "

JUMBLE®

Unscramble these four Jumbles, one letter to each square, to form four ordinary words.

TEJEC

KESTO

BAHCLE

GRANAH

HE MISSES HIS WIFE'S COOKING---

Now arrange the circled letters to form the surprise answer, as suggested by the above cartoon.

Print answer here EVERY ⃝⃝⃝⃝⃝⃝ HE ⃝⃝⃝⃝

133

JUMBLE®

Unscramble these four Jumbles, one letter to each square, to form four ordinary words.

NOBAT

RUPUS

LONPEL

UNGOAT

Ignorance is bliss

THAT OPINIONATED GUY WAS ALWAYS DOWN ON ANY-THING ---

Now arrange the circled letters to form the surprise answer, as suggested by the above cartoon.

Print answer here HE WAS ☐☐☐ " ☐☐ " ☐☐

134

JUMBLE®

Unscramble these four Jumbles, one letter to each square, to form four ordinary words.

SEROU

TEELA

REVOND

GREDLE

SOME PEOPLE, WHEN THEY "HOLD" A CONVERSATION---

Now arrange the circled letters to form the surprise answer, as suggested by the above cartoon.

Print answer here

JUMBLE®

Unscramble these four Jumbles, one letter to each square, to form four ordinary words.

VENET

OONES

NERKUB

SHURTH

No wonder he's number one!

And all those commercials!

THEY WERE IN THE MILLIONS!

Now arrange the circled letters to form the surprise answer, as suggested by the above cartoon.

Print answer here   HIS ☐☐☐ ☐☐☐☐☐☐☐☐

JUMBLE®

Unscramble these four Jumbles, one letter to each square, to form four ordinary words.

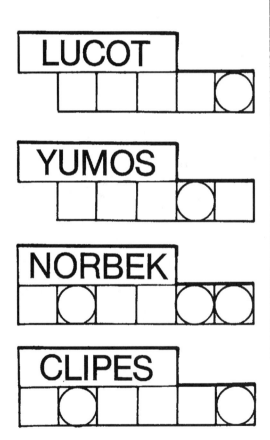

LUCOT

YUMOS

NORBEK

CLIPES

WHAT EVE FIGURED THAT SHE WAS GETTING FROM THE SERPENT.

Now arrange the circled letters to form the surprise answer, as suggested by the above cartoon.

Print answer here A "◯◯◯◯◯◯◯"

137

JUMBLE®

Unscramble these four Jumbles, one letter to each square, to form four ordinary words.

LAVNA

YATTS

MAGITS

URIADS

Looks like gridlock

THE REGATTA WAS SO FULL OF SAILBOATS THAT IT MADE ONE THINK OF THIS.

Now arrange the circled letters to form the surprise answer, as suggested by the above cartoon.

Print answer here " ⬡⬡⬡⬡ " ⬡⬡⬡⬡⬡⬡⬡

JUMBLE®

Unscramble these four Jumbles, one letter to each square, to form four ordinary words.

MYHRE

LUTEX

SAFRAC

THRAHE

THE OPINIONATED GUY DIDN'T WANT TO BE CONFUSED BY THIS.

Now arrange the circled letters to form the surprise answer, as suggested by the above cartoon.

Print answer here

JUMBLE®

Unscramble these four Jumbles, one letter to each square, to form four ordinary words.

BALOT

NAVER

DOWMIS

CUPHAN

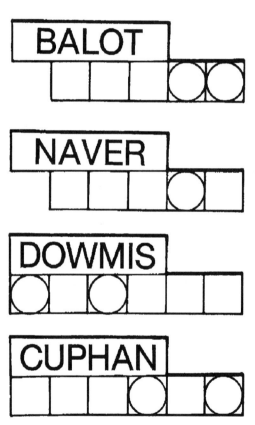

Four more takeovers— and your new yacht just arrived!

But he never gets any fun out of life

HE NEVER NEEDS AS MUCH AS ---

Now arrange the circled letters to form the surprise answer, as suggested by the above cartoon.

Print answer here

140

JUMBLE®

Unscramble these four Jumbles, one letter to each square, to form four ordinary words.

PONCA

TRYNE

UNSLIM

GEDDUR

And now for the storybook ending

HE DOESN'T UNDERSTAND THAT HIS WIFE DOES---

Now arrange the circled letters to form the surprise answer, as suggested by the above cartoon.

Print answer here ⬡⬡⬡⬡⬡⬡⬡⬡⬡⬡ HIM

JUMBLE®

Unscramble these four Jumbles, one letter to
each square, to form four ordinary words.

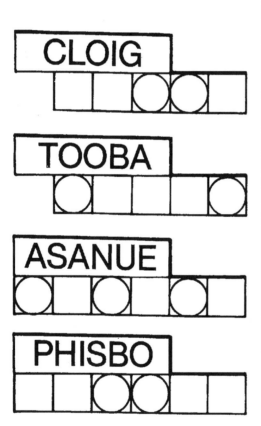

CLOIG

TOOBA

ASANUE

PHISBO

Keep this in confidence...

THAT SECRET AGENT COULDN'T HOLD ONTO HIS JOB BECAUSE HE COULDN'T HOLD THIS.

Now arrange the circled letters to form
the surprise answer, as suggested by the
above cartoon.

Print answer here

142

JUMBLE®

Unscramble these four Jumbles, one letter to each square, to form four ordinary words.

CHIRB

FYFAT

SLICHE

RAHPON

IT WAS THE TALK OF PARIS!

Now arrange the circled letters to form the surprise answer, as suggested by the above cartoon.

Print answer here " ◯◯◯◯◯◯ "

143

JUMBLE®

Unscramble these four Jumbles, one letter to each square, to form four ordinary words.

YOGGS

CHAVO

GREATT

VISTEN

A PEDESTRIAN IS A PERSON WHO HAS LEARNED THAT IT DOESN'T ALWAYS PAY TO ---

Now arrange the circled letters to form the surprise answer, as suggested by the above cartoon.

Print answer here

JUMBLE®

Unscramble these four Jumbles, one letter to each square, to form four ordinary words.

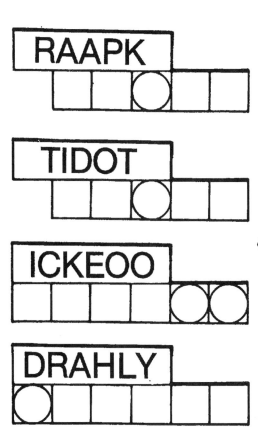

RAAPK

TIDOT

ICKEOO

DRAHLY

Marvin and I are teeing off at eight tomorrow

OH, NO YOU'RE NOT

THEY BECOME POSSESSIVE.

Now arrange the circled letters to form the surprise answer, as suggested by the above cartoon.

Print answer here

JUMBLE®

Unscramble these four Jumbles, one letter to each square, to form four ordinary words.

DEKIN

CUDIL

SWACHE

TRIVED

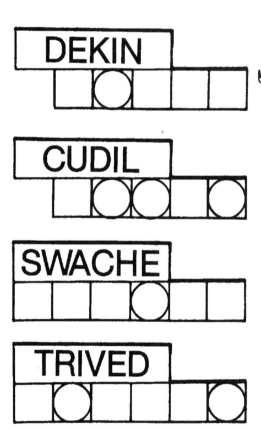

WHAT THOSE TOURISTS GOT WHILE IN HOLLAND.

Now arrange the circled letters to form the surprise answer, as suggested by the above cartoon.

Print answer here

JUMBLE®

Unscramble these four Jumbles, one letter to each square, to form four ordinary words.

NELOB

GUJED

LEZZUP

SIFOSY

WHERE YOU USUALLY ARE WHEN THE ALARM MAKES THAT SOUND.

Now arrange the circled letters to form the surprise answer, as suggested by the above cartoon.

Print answer here IN A

JUMBLE®

Unscramble these four Jumbles, one letter to each square, to form four ordinary words.

USSEO

HISFY

JELIGG

THEIRZ

He puts a lot of effort into this business

He'll be filthy rich in no time

GUYS WHO REGULARLY ROLL UP THEIR SLEEVES AT WORK SELDOM DO THIS.

Now arrange the circled letters to form the surprise answer, as suggested by the above cartoon.

Print answer here ⬭⬭⬭⬭ THEIR ⬭⬭⬭⬭⬭⬭

JUMBLE®

Unscramble these four Jumbles, one letter to each square, to form four ordinary words.

PERIT

FRACT

TAILIC

NAPMEN

OUR CAT LIKES A CATNAP AFTER THIS.

Now arrange the circled letters to form the surprise answer, as suggested by the above cartoon.

Print answer here A ☐☐☐ AT THE ☐☐☐☐☐☐

149

JUMBLE®

Unscramble these four Jumbles, one letter to each square, to form four ordinary words.

PRAAT

YENEM

STIGAR

LUSHIM

WHAT THE CRITIC SAID WHEN THE BUTCHER TOOK UP SERIOUS ACTING.

Now arrange the circled letters to form the surprise answer, as suggested by the above cartoon.

Print answer here NEVER " ◯◯◯◯◯◯◯ " A ◯◯◯

JUMBLE®

Unscramble these four Jumbles, one letter to each square, to form four ordinary words.

AMWAC

NOYOL

HECREY

CINORI

Oops! Have to stop off here

What's so important?

Fine Jewelry

HOW OFTEN DOES A HUSBAND FORGET AN ANNIVERSARY?

Now arrange the circled letters to form the surprise answer, as suggested by the above cartoon.

Print answer here

151

JUMBLE®

Unscramble these four Jumbles, one letter to each square, to form four ordinary words.

THONC

HOCEK

PEROOC

MOOSER

WHAT DOES YOUR DOG GIVE YOU THAT NO ONE ELSE CAN?

Now arrange the circled letters to form the surprise answer, as suggested by the above cartoon.

Print answer here   A

JUMBLE®

Unscramble these four Jumbles, one letter to each square, to form four ordinary words.

CANKS

ROPAN

DOUBEY

THAAMS

AT THAT EXPENSIVE NIGHTCLUB ALL THE TABLES WERE RESERVED, BUT NOT THIS.

Now arrange the circled letters to form the surprise answer, as suggested by the above cartoon.

Print answer here   THE ◯◯◯◯◯◯◯◯◯◯

JUMBLE®

Unscramble these four Jumbles, one letter to each square, to form four ordinary words.

CEKEH

DYNAD

TRAIPY

CAUVIN

WHAT ONE POLAR EXPLORER SAID TO THE OTHER.

Now arrange the circled letters to form the surprise answer, as suggested by the above cartoon.

Print answer here ☐☐☐☐☐ AN ☐☐☐☐☐☐

154

JUMBLE®

Unscramble these four Jumbles, one letter to
each square, to form four ordinary words.

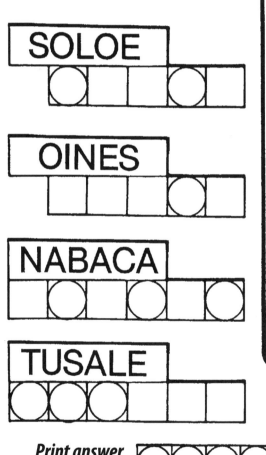

SOLOE

OINES

NABACA

TUSALE

Maternity

WHAT THE FATHER
OF TEN GIRLS
SAID WHEN YET
ANOTHER ARRIVED.

Now arrange the circled letters to form
the surprise answer, as suggested by the
above cartoon.

**Print answer
here**

155

JUMBLE®

Unscramble these four Jumbles, one letter to each square, to form four ordinary words.

BETER

DICAR

CHOTEL

INGEEN

Vote for me and I'll guarantee higher taxes and more unemployment

POLITICAL JOKES AREN'T ALWAYS FUNNY, ESPECIALLY WHEN THEY---

Now arrange the circled letters to form the surprise answer, as suggested by the above cartoon.

Print answer here

JUMBLE®

Unscramble these four Jumbles, one letter to
each square, to form four ordinary words.

LOVEC

DUFAR

MAIRDY

SAYQUE

HURRY WITH YOUR
MAKEUP, DEAR, OR
WE'LL BE LATE

Now arrange the circled letters to form
the surprise answer, as suggested by the
above cartoon.

Print answer here " " ☐☐☐☐☐ " IN A ☐☐☐ "

JUMBLE®

Unscramble these four Jumbles, one letter to each square, to form four ordinary words.

NOONI

PLYAP

RACLIG

ZEEMAC

I-I-I-er-ah---

A SPOUSE CAN ALWAYS GET IN THE LAST WORD WHEN IT'S THIS.

Now arrange the circled letters to form the surprise answer, as suggested by the above cartoon.

Print answer here " ◯◯◯◯◯◯◯◯◯◯ "

158

JUMBLE®

Unscramble these four Jumbles, one letter to each square, to form four ordinary words.

DARAW

SURNP

CODJUN

PAFFOY

WHAT THEY SAID EVERY TIME DAD CAME UP WITH ONE OF HIS STALE JOKES.

Now arrange the circled letters to form the surprise answer, as suggested by the above cartoon.

Print answer here "◯◯◯ --- ◯◯◯◯!"

159

JUMBLE®

Unscramble these four Jumbles, one letter to each square, to form four ordinary words.

GOROF

RIBAN

CAMIAN

TIPEOA

WHERE DID THE OLD LADY WHO LIVED IN A SHOE SEND HER KIDS WHEN THEY GREW UP?

Now arrange the circled letters to form the surprise answer, as suggested by the above cartoon.

Print answer here   TO " ◯◯◯◯◯ " ◯◯◯◯

JUMBLE®

Unscramble these four Jumbles, one letter to each square, to form four ordinary words.

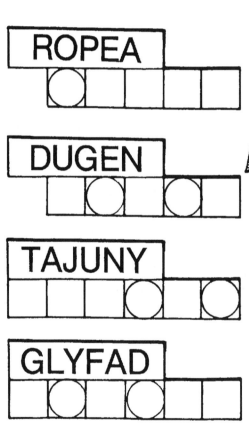

ROPEA

DUGEN

TAJUNY

GLYFAD

WHAT DRACULA PO—LITELY SAID, AFTER ENJOYING HIS USUAL GUSTATORY TREATS.

Now arrange the circled letters to form the surprise answer, as suggested by the above cartoon.

Print answer here " ◯◯◯◯ " ◯◯◯

161

JUMBLE®

Unscramble these four Jumbles, one letter to each square, to form four ordinary words.

GNAAP

SEHCS

DANGIE

YUIRPT

I think she misunderstood

SHE SAID SHE WAS EXPECTING TO BECOME ENGAGED, BECAUSE HER BOYFRIEND TOLD HER HE'D GIVE HER THIS.

Now arrange the circled letters to form the surprise answer, as suggested by the above cartoon.

Print answer here A ◯◯◯◯ ONE ◯◯◯◯◯

162

MONSTER JUMBLE®

Challenger Puzzles

JUMBLE®

Unscramble these six Jumbles, one letter to each square, to form six ordinary words.

IFTIEN

HCPTYA

ENMYOK

FINEUS

TTYNWE

GNEAEG

We're getting orders from all over the U.S.

The iSWEEPINATOR 2000

We can have that to you in Hawaii by next week.

HIS NEW PATENTED BROOM WAS SUCH A SUCCESS THAT IT WAS THIS.

Now arrange the circled letters to form the surprise answer, as suggested by the above cartoon.

Print answer here

THE

164

JUMBLE®

Unscramble these six Jumbles, one letter to each square, to form six ordinary words.

DALPED

CNECAT

SELNUS

ROSWOR

THOOMS

GHILPT

LEFTORIUM Syd's Cakes Kathy K Designs

Please Use Stairs

JUMBLE STORE

STAIRS

Meet Jumble's David & Jeff Tonight!

I thought we fixed this last week.

It's great when the escalator is working, but lately it seems to be broken most of the time.

Not In SERVICE

THE MALL'S NEW ESCALATOR HAD ----

Now arrange the circled letters to form the surprise answer, as suggested by the above cartoon.

Print answer here

JUMBLE

Unscramble these six Jumbles, one letter to each square, to form six ordinary words.

CEESUX

LOPWIL

BUNYOT

VIDCAE

DALHYR

PECACT

My journey will open trade routes to China. And it will be very profitable for you, if you invest.

That's some risky travel ahead of you.

IF MARCO POLO HAD NEEDED MONEY FOR HIS EPIC JOURNEY, HE COULD HAVE RAISED ----

Now arrange the circled letters to form the surprise answer, as suggested by the above cartoon.

Print answer here

JUMBLE®

Unscramble these six Jumbles, one letter to each square, to form six ordinary words.

YEGRES

MOTSED

FENTIC

RIOHAD

CIPCIN

EXTROV

I'm glad we had the camera rolling. All of my online friends can now see it .

Great catch.

THE SHORT MOVIE HE POSTED OF HIMSELF CATCHING A HUGE TROUT WAS A ---

Now arrange the circled letters to form the surprise answer, as suggested by the above cartoon.

Print answer here

JUMBLE®

Unscramble these six Jumbles, one letter to each square, to form six ordinary words.

CHLOTB

WORDYS

LUWSAR

SAGTEK

FUNIRA

PIBOSH

Here you are! I thought you weren't working this week!

I'm not. Sketching is just so relaxing!

THE JUMBLE CARTOONIST SPENT HIS VACATION ----

Now arrange the circled letters to form the surprise answer, as suggested by the above cartoon.

Print answer here

JUMBLE®

Unscramble these six Jumbles, one letter to each square, to form six ordinary words.

WOSMID

BAHSYB

NIMGEL

TINHEZ

TEPTON

TOLINO

I need to get out of here, fast!

THE TEAM'S TOUCHDOWN DRIVE ENDED WHEN THEY DROVE INTO A ----

Now arrange the circled letters to form the surprise answer, as suggested by the above cartoon.

Print answer here

JUMBLE®

Unscramble these six Jumbles, one letter to each square, to form six ordinary words.

NIDLAS

CRONEE

TREESO

DOANUR

FAITNN

RULPEY

Hey, Jeff, I'm drawing a blank. I just can't seem to come up with anything for the Sunday puzzle.

The deadline's today. What do you want me to draw? I can't draw a blank because you're "drawing a blank."

I ♥ JUMBLE

AFTER THE JUMBLE PUZZLE MAKER SAID HE WAS AT A LOSS FOR WORDS, HE SAID ---

Now arrange the circled letters to form the surprise answer, as suggested by the above cartoon.

Print answer here

JUMBLE

Unscramble these six Jumbles, one letter to each square, to form six ordinary words.

CLINEY

TINEBT

CULONK

INSECK

SMOBYL

SPOPEO

Shouldn't they be working?

This is the way they work.

Surf's up, Davy!

Let's try it again from the top.

Looks like I have the shakes.

Anyone have an eraser?

WHEN JONES, TORK, DOLENZ AND NESMITH TEAMED UP, EVERYONE ENJOYED THEIR ----

Now arrange the circled letters to form the surprise answer, as suggested by the above cartoon.

Print answer here

" ◯◯◯◯◯◯ " ◯◯◯◯◯◯◯◯◯

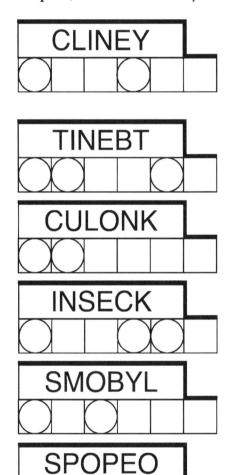

JUMBLE

Unscramble these six Jumbles, one letter to each square, to form six ordinary words.

DEYOMB

PLIPUT

SALPRU

VISENT

ARTREH

UTEDAP

I don't have enough for the down payment.

I'm not sure you're allowed to live there.

For Sale OFFICERS ONLY

THE ENLISTED SOLDIER WANTED TO BUY REAL ESTATE, BUT HE COULDN'T AFFORD ---

Now arrange the circled letters to form the surprise answer, as suggested by the above cartoon.

Print answer here

172

JUMBLE

Unscramble these six Jumbles, one letter to each square, to form six ordinary words.

ACIFOS

BMEMEL

TEBLOT

ELAFME

ENURSU

HPYENH

Jeff! Jeff! Where are you?

Hey. Isn't that your wife?

Huh?

SHE COULDN'T FIND HER HUSBAND IN THE CASINO. HE WENT TO PLAY POKER, BUT GOT ---

Now arrange the circled letters to form the surprise answer, as suggested by the above cartoon.

Print answer here

⬡⬡⬡⬡ ⬡⬡ ⬡⬡⬡ ⬡⬡⬡⬡⬡⬡⬡

JUMBLE®

Unscramble these six Jumbles, one letter to
each square, to form six ordinary words.

DRAUWP

RETHOB

BITSUM

YALMIN

NATQUI

CORVEL

WHAT THEY CALLED
THAT MUCH ARMED
DEEP - SEA BANDIT.

Now arrange the circled letters to form
the surprise answer, as suggested by
the above cartoon.

Print answer here

174

JUMBLE

Unscramble these six Jumbles, one letter to each square, to form six ordinary words.

CHORCT

TREOTT

DAZIOC

ONBOAB

LETTEK

MELLUV

WHAT THE BARGAIN SALE AT THE DEPARTMENT STORE WAS.

Now arrange the circled letters to form the surprise answer, as suggested by the above cartoon.

Print answer here

A " "

175

JUMBLE®

Unscramble these six Jumbles, one letter to
each square, to form six ordinary words.

LUFNIX

HAIDAL

SCETOK

CRYLEE

LOGYOM

NIWWON

What a lovely
promenade

WHERE THIS FORM
OF EXERCISE
IS POPULAR.

Now arrange the circled letters to form
the surprise answer, as suggested by
the above cartoon.

Print answer here

IN ⬡⬡⬡ ⬡⬡⬡⬡⬡ OF ⬡⬡⬡⬡

176

JUMBLE®

Unscramble these six Jumbles, one letter to each square, to form six ordinary words.

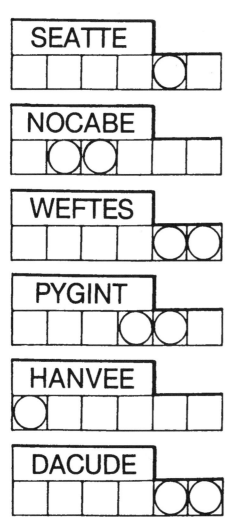

SEATTE

NOCABE

WEFTES

PYGINT

HANVEE

DACUDE

A GREAT COMPOSER INVOLVED WITH SURGERY.

Now arrange the circled letters to form the surprise answer, as suggested by the above cartoon.

Print answer here

AN

JUMBLE®

Unscramble these six Jumbles, one letter to each square, to form six ordinary words.

STURME

TOLBEG

RAYNPT

AUVEEN

GEDDER

DIMPEE

HAMBURGER JOINT

WHAT STARTED AS BEEF ON THE HOOF ENDED UP AS THIS.

Now arrange the circled letters to form the surprise answer, as suggested by the above cartoon.

Print answer here

THE ◯◯◯◯ "◯◯◯◯◯◯◯-◯◯"

JUMBLE®

Unscramble these six Jumbles, one letter to each square, to form six ordinary words.

MORTER

GARNAL

SUCLEM

AURBUE

LANSID

WOAMED

I couldn't care less

IF THAT SNOBBISH HORSE IS FINICKY ABOUT HIS HAY, TELL HIM YOU'RE SERVING THIS.

Now arrange the circled letters to form the surprise answer, as suggested by the above cartoon.

Print answer here

◯◯◯◯◯ ◯ LA " ◯◯◯◯◯ "

179

JUMBLE®

Unscramble these six Jumbles, one letter to each square, to form six ordinary words.

BOCHOR

YECTIN

HAUTOR

CAMEEN

ACDAFE

TESVIN

You're on a diet!

MIGHT HELP LENGTHEN YOUR LIFE IF YOU LEARN TO DO THIS.

Now arrange the circled letters to form the surprise answer, as suggested by the above cartoon.

Print answer here

☐☐☐☐☐☐☐☐ YOUR ☐☐☐☐☐

180

JUMBLE®

Unscramble these six Jumbles, one letter to each square, to form six ordinary words.

ERKLAT

VINTIE

SOOPPE

WARMOR

ZULZEG

PANNKI

That's a cheerful earful

WHAT THEY GAVE THE SINGER.

Now arrange the circled letters to form the surprise answer, as suggested by the above cartoon.

Print answer here

THE " ⬡⬡⬡⬡ " OF ⬡⬡⬡⬡⬡⬡⬡⬡

181

JUMBLE®

Unscramble these six Jumbles, one letter to each square, to form six ordinary words.

YOANNE

MENECT

CIPCIN

GOTHET

FLEMSY

BIMBIE

WILL THESE STEPS TAKE ME TO THE CAPITOL?

Now arrange the circled letters to form the surprise answer, as suggested by the above cartoon.

Print answer here

" ◯◯, YOU HAVE TO ◯◯◯◯◯◯ ◯◯◯◯◯ "

JUMBLE®

Unscramble these six Jumbles, one letter to each square, to form six ordinary words.

GRAULF

RUBETT

TARROM

SEATTE

PELPIN

OTHPRY

WHAT THERE WERE WHEN THAT POMPOUS FOOL SLIPPED ON A BANANA.

Now arrange the circled letters to form the surprise answer, as suggested by the above cartoon.

Print answer here

" ❍❍❍❍❍ " OF ❍❍❍❍❍❍❍❍❍

183

Answers

1. **Jumbles:** CARGO ELOPE BITTER DETACH
   Answer: For some people, global warming is a—HEATED TOPIC

2. **Jumbles:** EVOKE RAYON FELONY HERMIT
   Answer: Business was good, but the policeman only wanted to—FINE ART

3. **Jumbles:** CUBIC HABIT SKIMPY INDOOR
   Answer: The archaeologist wished the caveman was still alive so he could—PICK HIS BRAIN

4. **Jumbles:** IMPEL PURGE TRUDGE FIASCO
   Answer: When they added ornaments to the Christmas tree, they—SPRUCED IT UP

5. **Jumbles:** WAFER ADAPT HOURLY ZODIAC
   Answer: He puts up so many Christmas lights, the neighbors were in a—"HOLI-DAZE"

6. **Jumbles:** UNWED OCCUR REBUKE FORGOT
   Answer: The Empire was able to get another Death Star built quickly, thanks to the—WORKFORCE

7. **Jumbles:** CABIN OPERA DOODLE OUTAGE
   Answer: The wide receiver's wedding day featured a—GOOD RECEPTION

8. **Jumbles:** MOVIE KAYAK COWARD SKIMPY
   Answer: Yogi and Boo-Boo were taking karate lessons and Yogi was impressed with his—SIDEKICK

9. **Jumbles:** MOUTH OFFER IMPACT BOTANY
   Answer: He proposed a submarine to reach the bottom of the ocean, but his boss couldn't—FATHOM IT

10. **Jumbles:** LEAVE POUND LIZARD PHOBIA
    Answer: New Year's Eve would be problem-free, as long as someone—DROPPED THE BALL

11. **Jumbles:** ADMIT DICEY JARGON DROWSY
    Answer: He made such a good archer because he understood—ARROW-DYNAMICS

12. **Jumbles:** VERGE CRUSH AGENCY INTENT
    Answer: The tennis player was double-faulting way too much, so he went to a—SERVICE CENTER

13. **Jumbles:** DITTO DODGE RANCID PONCHO
    Answer: The school's new math teacher was a—GOOD ADDITION

14. **Jumbles:** JUICE EVENT SCROLL FILLET
    Answer: When the clown helped out the ringmaster, he was a—NICE JESTER

15. **Jumbles:** IMAGE DITTO UNJUST GLANCE
    Answer: He wasn't sure exactly how many people were staying at the hotel, so he—"GUEST-IMATED"

16. **Jumbles:** OOMPH ENACT SUNKEN IGUANA
    Answer: After not being called safe, the baseball player was—OUTSPOKEN

17. **Jumbles:** OUNCE DERBY VENDOR OUTLAW
    Answer: Peter Pan couldn't fight Captain Hook because his punches would—NEVER LAND

18. **Jumbles:** GIZMO TROLL MUTINY FOSSIL
    Answer: If you asked Tolstoy why "War and Peace" had 1,225 pages, he'd say it was a—LONG STORY

19. **Jumbles:** RANCH FOYER HAPPEN SOCIAL
    Answer: The trumpeter couldn't find a replacement trumpet in Paris because they only sold—FRENCH HORNS

20. **Jumbles:** EXCEL SPELL SHROUD BOUNTY
    Answer: When the cyclops moved into the neighborhood, his messy yard was an—EYESORE

21. **Jumbles:** HOIST MONEY NEATLY RADISH
    Answer: When he was arrested, the mime chose to—REMAIN SILENT

22. **Jumbles:** PLANT GLOAT RADIUS FOURTH
    Answer: They parachuted together on a regular basis until they had a—FALLING OUT

23. **Jumbles:** BUDDY AFTER PULPIT EXCESS
    Answer: He was this after hearing the details of his job severance package—FIRED UP

24. **Jumbles:** WEARY BUILD GENTLE ENZYME
    Answer: They bought the discounted sunglasses after seeing that they were—"EYE-DEAL"

25. **Jumbles:** ZESTY ABOUT DROWSY RICHLY
    Answer: J.K. Rowling noticed some charges on her credit card bill that weren't—"AUTHOR-IZED"

26. **Jumbles:** CABIN ARBOR AFLAME ITALIC
    Answer: The cost to change his flight was going to be $600. He didn't think that was—"AIR-FAIR"

27. **Jumbles:** WINCE GIDDY EXPERT CAMERA
    Answer: She planned to work in her garden until she—GREW TIRED

28. **Jumbles:** ROBOT BATTY IGUANA ENSIGN
    Answer: He bought the tavern because it was a—BAR-GAIN

29. **Jumbles:** ADAPT CLAMP SHRIMP FONDLY
    Answer: The architect couldn't stay for the meeting because he—HAD PLANS

30. **Jumbles:** PROUD SHYLY BOTHER ASTRAY
    Answer: The law student declined going to the tavern so he could—PASS THE BAR

31. **Jumbles:** SPOIL GROUP TANDEM INTACT
    Answer: When they offered her a chance to advertise on the billboard at a discount, she said—SIGN ME UP

32. **Jumbles:** GOUGE HOUSE EXTENT CANNED
    Answer: The bat bar was becoming a popular—HANGOUT

33. **Jumbles:** INEPT SCOUT GAMBLE HUDDLE
    Answer: The funeral home director read his book in—DEAD SILENCE

34. **Jumbles:** PANIC SEEDY REGRET OBLONG
    Answer: The animal band needed a new drummer, so they hired—DINGO STARR

35. **Jumbles:** NUDGE HABIT INLAND HOOPLA
    Answer: Falling in love and going for walks together—GO HAND-IN-HAND

36. **Jumbles:** KOALA EVENT FEISTY HAIRDO
    Answer: The horse wasn't feeling well because of—HAY FEVER

37. **Jumbles:** SNIFF AGENT DIVIDE BOTTOM
    Answer: The student forgot to go to school because he was—ABSENT-MINDED

38. **Jumbles:** SHOWN FAULT EXCITE SCULPT
    Answer: The greedy owner of the seafood market was—"SELL-FISH"

39. **Jumbles:** OOMPH OCCUR LAWFUL AUTUMN
    Answer: After a long day of showing off the new clothing line, the fashion model was—WORN OUT

40. **Jumbles:** SLUSH ALBUM BETRAY ADRIFT
    Answer: To win the Green Jacket at Augusta, a golfer needs to play—MASTERFULLY

41. **Jumbles:** UNFIT MOUND INTENT ALKALI
    Answer: His passion for high-calorie food was—INFATUATION

42. **Jumbles:** SLANT INPUT FONDUE MAGNET
    Answer: When the pioneers learned that their homestead was a swamp, the news was—UNSETTLING

43. **Jumbles:** RIGOR GEESE ACTIVE COBALT
    Answer: The retriever's store was so successful because he was a—REAL GO-GETTER

44. **Jumbles:** WHILE FLINT INDUCT HARDER
Answer: He wasn't exactly sure what was wrong with the violin and needed to—FIDDLE WITH IT

45. **Jumbles:** YIELD BOGUS UNLOCK PLEDGE
Answer: The new discount store was—CLOSE "BUY"

46. **Jumbles:** HAVOC TEMPT RADIUS MIFFED
Answer: The dog thought the idea of retrieving the ball was—FAR-FETCHED

47. **Jumbles:** AWARE MINUS SHADOW TEACUP
Answer: The sign on the ladies' room at the horse ranch said—"WHOA-MEN"

48. **Jumbles:** AHEAD YUCKY IRONIC BICKER
Answer: The wild ox did so well in school because he was a—"BRAINY-YAK"

49. **Jumbles:** EVOKE RIGID APATHY TEDIUM
Answer: They wanted a purebred dog with a great bloodline, but they couldn't—"PET-AGREE"

50. **Jumbles:** DOUSE RANCH POUNCE CHOOSE
Answer: The new prison had its—PROS AND CONS

51. **Jumbles:** IMPEL KNACK PULLEY RELENT
Answer: When they got caught in the downpour in Kiev, they were in the—"UK-RAIN-E"

52. **Jumbles:** MOGUL RELIC CHOSEN FLIGHT
Answer: He was called for being offsides so often because he kept—RUSHING

53. **Jumbles:** STUNG DROLL PRANCE OUTLAW
Answer: Trading in his old cell phone for a new one was— A GOOD CALL

54. **Jumbles:** TROLL DIVOT EITHER ASTRAY
Answer: He had his bowling ball and bowling shoes… he was—READY TO ROLL

55. **Jumbles:** ZESTY ARROW POISON IRONIC
Answer: When their commanding officer won an award, it was a—"SIR-PRIZE"

56. **Jumbles:** AFOOT DAZED SKETCH AUTUMN
Answer: After seeing his new co-worker at the calendar factory he wanted to—MAKE A DATE

57. **Jumbles:** HAVOC CABIN NUMBER LIZARD
Answer: Going fishing made it possible for the TV reporter to become—AN ANCHORMAN

58. **Jumbles:** LEAVE ZESTY JOGGER MAGPIE
Answer: When King Kong escaped from custody, he was— AT LARGE

59. **Jumbles:** BRAWN JOINT INLAND MUSKET
Answer: To the new technician working at the sleep study institute was—A DREAM JOB

60. **Jumbles:** VENUE TRACT MODULE HYBRID
Answer: Fishing when the water was low would have to— TIDE THEM OVER

61. **Jumbles:** AWAIT GLADE GROUND INDIGO
Answer: The runner tried to make it to third base, but unfortunately for him, the shortstop—TAGGED ALONG

62. **Jumbles:** TIGER ADMIT STRAND PUZZLE
Answer: The circus performer painted during his time off because he was—TRAPEZE ARTIST

63. **Jumbles:** ROUND BRAVE SOCKET GALAXY
Answer: The sale on the firewood allowed the camper to— SAVE A BUNDLE

64. **Jumbles:** MODEM PRAWN GALON ROOKIE
Answer: When he didn't understand what was said at the parole hearing, the prisoner said—PARDON ME

65. **Jumbles:** SPURN PORCH DETACH ROSIER
Answer: If they were going to afford the new sailboat, they'd need—A PARTNER-SHIP

66. **Jumbles:** RUGBY VIDEO SUBMIT ROTATE
Answer: The billboard featured—AD VERBS

67. **Jumbles:** GRIPE MOURN BOTTOM WEAKEN
Answer: Her attempt to make her teenage son get a part-time job was—NOT WORKING

68. **Jumbles:** CRANK TITHE CLOSER DISMAY
Answer: The new employee was unhappy on his first payday because he got a—REALITY CHECK

69. **Jumbles:** CRAMP MORON ONWARD PUNDIT
Answer: What the zookeeper witnessed in the Asian animal section.—"PANDA-MONIUM"

70. **Jumbles:** GUILT WHEEL COPPER FROSTY
Answer: When her priceless Ming vase crashed to the floor, she—FELL TO PIECES

71. **Jumbles:** MONEY SCARF PROFIT GALLEY
Answer: The screenwriters didn't work well together because they couldn't get—ON THE SAME PAGE

72. **Jumbles:** CLOUT PERCH ACCORD FEEBLE
Answer: She didn't like coffee because it wasn't this— HER CUP OF TEA

73. **Jumbles:** HONOR FAULT GALLON HUNGRY
Answer: On July 3, 1776, the founding fathers decided that they should—GO "FOURTH"

74. **Jumbles:** WOUND UNFIT DENOTE AURORA
Answer: After his unsuccessful attempt to steal second, the player was this—DOWN AND OUT

75. **Jumbles:** GOOSE TOXIC TRUANT CASHEW
Answer: The performer struggled until he got his— ACT TOGETHER

76. **Jumbles:** BOOTH CLOTH TWELVE DAWNED
Answer: He was going to run for president, but in the end he—ELECTED NOT TO

77. **Jumbles:** MONTH TOKEN WALLOP PIGSTY
Answer: After finally finishing the mural, the artist wanted to do this—PAINT THE TOWN

78. **Jumbles:** SHINY WAFER UNLOCK BOUNCE
Answer: Her visit to the eye doctor was over in the— BLINK OF AN EYE

79. **Jumbles:** RIGID AVOID REGRET CATTLE
Answer: After he trained by running, cycling and swimming, the athlete decided to—GIVE IT A "TRI"

80. **Jumbles:** MESSY WHARF HIDDEN BICEPS
Answer: He was this as a result of his booming airboat business—SWAMPED

81. **Jumbles:** CABIN BRAND GAMBIT BEDBUG
Answer: What were they playing at the purse counter?— GRAB BAG

82. **Jumbles:** YOUTH CHIME DEBATE NICETY
Answer: How she arrived at her destination—BY ACCIDENT

83. **Jumbles:** IGLOO AORTA PAUNCH DISCUS
Answer: They contract to give you a comfortable ride— SPRINGS

84. **Jumbles:** WOMEN ENEMY BEHELD HANGER
Answer: What a doctor puts on before he starts working— AN "M D"

85. **Jumbles:** BEFIT VOCAL MARKUP FROTHY
Answer: What they said when they held up the shop— FORK IT OVER

86. **Jumbles:** MILKY CURVE FUNGUS ABSURD
Answer: This calls for the army!—A BUGLE

87. **Jumbles:** SHINY COUGH CHOSEN BEAUTY
Answer: What the team didn't have when it lost its "spirit"— A GHOST OF A CHANCE

88. **Jumbles:** UNIFY GUISE SECEDE FRACAS
Answer: Those who take it are out for the count—CENSUS

89. **Jumbles:** WEIGH FOCUS PESTLE FINALE
Answer: People would expect their support from cradle to grave—LEGS

185

90. **Jumbles:** PILOT INLET BELFRY SLOGAN
Answer: What they called the British beef tycoon—"SIR LOIN"

91. **Jumbles:** FLOUR BOGUS PONDER DARING
Answer: They often go out to sea in ports—PIERS

92. **Jumbles:** DRAMA SAUTE DEFACE HUMBLE
Answer: He said this was the acting game—CHARADES

93. **Jumbles:** CEASE PANSY LOTION BLOUSE
Answer: Take in hand for a bath!—SOAP

94. **Jumbles:** MINCE HEDGE DEVOUR NEGATE
Answer: A kind of surreptitious ball playing—"UNDERHAND"

95. **Jumbles:** OUNCE MANLY STOLID MYSTIC
Answer: In a word, it means the same thing!—SYNONYM

96. **Jumbles:** ABHOR STOIC FLIMSY DETAIN
Answer: The best part of the theater—THE STAR'S

97. **Jumbles:** ANNUL ROBIN PIRATE MOTION
Answer: MEN IN PORT are conspicuous—PROMINENT

98. **Jumbles:** IDIOM SPURN FIERCE AUTHOR
Answer: The back part of these weapons is in the center—"FI-REAR-MS"

99. **Jumbles:** CASTE FLAKE TROPHY OVERDO
Answer: It's against the law to pick them in parks—POCKETS

100. **Jumbles:** EMERY STAID SICKEN EXCITE
Answer: May discover a new star—A SCREEN TEST

101. **Jumbles:** BUILT MOUTH WEASEL RADIUM
Answer: What kind of waiter won't accept a tip?—A DUMB WAITER

102. **Jumbles:** RANCH DUCAT VOYAGE STIGMA
Answer: The kind of time she had shopping for a dress—"TRYING"

103. **Jumbles:** ITCHY AFOOT BOTANY FOMENT
Answer: What the fourth offender drunk had to be wary of—A FIFTH

104. **Jumbles:** CLEFT EXPEL WOEFUL HAIRDO
Answer: How the cobbler hoped to leave his family—WELL-HEELED

105. **Jumbles:** EJECT UNCLE FLORAL CACTUS
Answer: What the newly-married salad king begged the press to do—"LETTUCE" ALONE

106. **Jumbles:** POACH HAREM PANTRY WEAPON
Answer: What Lady Godiva said at the end of her ride—"WHOA"

107. **Jumbles:** ALIAS ICING AGENCY DEADLY
Answer: What the chicken farmer's prize entry did at the county fair—LAID AN EGG

108. **Jumbles:** BURST PROBE SMOKER SALUTE
Answer: What did they call the cat that fell into the pickle barrel?—A "SOUR PUSS"

109. **Jumbles:** CHUTE EXTOL SCENIC BICKER
Answer: The ladies in the sewing circle were—CLOSE KNIT

110. **Jumbles:** MINER SHEAF HOOKED DOUBLE
Answer: Something largely responsible for the pasta king's success—HIS NOODLE

111. **Jumbles:** KNEEL FLAME ANSWER BUTTON
Answer: You might be this when your apartment costs more than you can afford—FLAT BROKE

112. **Jumbles:** EXULT GLOAT BREACH AFLOAT
Answer: What the boxer was worried about—A BOUT

113. **Jumbles:** PIETY EVOKE FORMAT POLISH
Answer: What some people who run for offices probably did—OVERSLEPT

114. **Jumbles:** TARDY DOUSE BROGUE TREMOR
Answer: What dunking might be, besides being bad manners—GOOD TASTE

115. **Jumbles:** MAXIM INKED SATIRE DEVICE
Answer: What the terrible-tempered sugar grower did—RAISED CANE

116. **Jumbles:** ELEGY TOOTH CAVORT UNSAID
Answer: A person who makes little things count—A TEACHER

117. **Jumbles:** STEED IRATE GUNNER MARROW
Answer: What jaywalkers may be wearing tomorrow—WINGS

118. **Jumbles:** PAGAN DOWDY BEDECK FURROW
Answer: What a few catty remarks turned the ladies' lounge into—A POWDER KEG

119. **Jumbles:** TONIC NOVEL BLAZER FERRET
Answer: The manager said the pinch hitter would be a change—FOR THE "BATTER"

120. **Jumbles:** ENACT JUICY CONCUR TIPTOE
Answer: What a picnic with kids sometimes is—"NO PICNIC"

121. **Jumbles:** OPIUM PRINT SAVAGE HAMPER
Answer: When she wants her husband's opinion—SHE GIVES IT TO HIM

122. **Jumbles:** BATHE HURRY PLOWED CARNAL
Answer: Where the heavyweight championship was held—AT THE "PUNCH BOWL"

123. **Jumbles:** NEEDY BUILT DURESS ASSURE
Answer: He was carrying on a great love affair—UNASSISTED

124. **Jumbles:** BOGUS GROOM PRAYER TREMOR
Answer: What the former bodybuilder's torso became as he reached middle age—MORE SO

125. **Jumbles:** CHIDE ABYSS FICKLE PAUPER
Answer: He didn't believe in being superstitious because he thought it might bring him this—BAD LUCK

126. **Jumbles:** HENCE ABOVE VOLUME PALATE
Answer: What she said to her boyfriend—YOU "AUTO" BEHAVE

127. **Jumbles:** GAVEL CIVIL LARYNX FAUCET
Answer: Some people who go "all out" often end up—"ALL IN"

128. **Jumbles:** HELLO FRAME GOLFER MAROON
Answer: What the arrival of spring after a miserable winter should bring—"RE-LEAF"

129. **Jumbles:** NEWSY GOOSE SECEDE HEREBY
Answer: What it takes to "bridle" one's tongue—HORSE SENSE

130. **Jumbles:** ACUTE BROOK UPTOWN SHAKEN
Answer: How the ballplayer felt on an off day—OUT OF "WHACK"

131. **Jumbles:** EJECT STOKE BLEACH HANGAR
Answer: He misses his wife's cooking—EVERY CHANCE HE GETS

132. **Jumbles:** BATON USURP POLLEN NOUGAT
Answer: That opinionated guy was always down on anything—HE WAS NOT "UP" ON

133. **Jumbles:** ROUSE ELATE VENDOR LEDGER
Answer: Some people when they "hold" a conversation—NEVER LET GO

134. **Jumbles:** EVENT NOOSE BUNKER THRUSH
Answer: They were in the millions!—HIS NET RETURNS

135. **Jumbles:** CLOUT MOUSY BROKEN SPLICE
Answer: What Eve figured that she was getting from the serpent—A "PRESENT"

136. **Jumbles:** NAVAL TASTY STIGMA RADIUS
Answer: The regatta was so full of sailboats that it made one think of this—"MAST" TRANSIT

137. **Jumbles:** RHYME EXULT FRACAS HEARTH
Answer: The opinionated guy didn't want to be confused by this—THE FACTS

138. **Jumbles:** BLOAT RAVEN WISDOM PAUNCH
Answer: He never needs as much as—HE WANTS

139. **Jumbles:** CAPON ENTRY MUSLIN DRUDGE
Answer: He doesn't understand that his wife does—UNDERSTAND HIM

186

140. **Jumbles:** LOGIC TABOO NAUSEA BISHOP
Answer: That secret agent couldn't hold onto his job because he couldn't hold this—HIS TONGUE

141. **Jumbles:** BIRCH TAFFY CHISEL ORPHAN
Answer: It was the talk of Paris!—"FRENCH"

142. **Jumbles:** SOGGY HAVOC TARGET INVEST
Answer: A pedestrian is a person who has learned that it doesn't always pay to—GO STRAIGHT

143. **Jumbles:** PARKA DITTO COOKIE HARDLY
Answer: They become possessive—THEIR

144. **Jumbles:** INKED LUCID CASHEW DIVERT
Answer: What those tourists got while in Holland—IN DUTCH

145. **Jumbles:** NOBLE JUDGE PUZZLE OSSIFY
Answer: Where you usually are when the alarm makes that sound—IN A SOUND SLEEP

146. **Jumbles:** SOUSE FISHY JIGGLE ZITHER
Answer: Guys who regularly roll up their sleeves at work seldom do this—LOSE THEIR SHIRTS

147. **Jumbles:** TRIPE CRAFT ITALIC PENMAN
Answer: Our cat likes a catnap after this— A NIP AT THE CATNIP

148. **Jumbles:** APART ENEMY GRATIS MULISH
Answer: What the critic said when the butcher took up serious acting—NEVER SAUSAGE A HAM

149. **Jumbles:** MACAW LOONY CHEERY IRONIC
Answer: How often does a husband forget an anniversary?— ONCE

150. **Jumbles:** NOTCH CHOKE COOPER MOROSE
Answer: What does your dog give you that no one else can? —A POOCH SMOOCH

151. **Jumbles:** SNACK APRON BUOYED ASTHMA
Answer: At that expensive nightclub all the tables were reserved, but not this—THE CUSTOMERS

152. **Jumbles:** CHEEK DANDY PARITY VICUNA
Answer: What one polar explorer said to the other— HAVE AN ICE DAY

153. **Jumbles:** LOOSE NOISE CABANA SALUTE
Answer: What the father of ten girls said when yet another arrived—ALAS—A LASS

154. **Jumbles:** BERET ACRID CLOTHE ENGINE
Answer: Political jokes aren't always funny, especially when they—GET ELECTED

155. **Jumbles:** CLOVE FRAUD MYRIAD QUEASY
Answer: "Hurry with your makeup, dear, or we'll be late"— "'REDDY' IN A SEC"

156. **Jumbles:** ONION APPLY GARLIC ECZEMA
Answer: A spouse can always get in the last word when it's this—"APOLOGIZE"

157. **Jumbles:** AWARD SPURN JOCUND PAYOFF
Answer: What they said every time dad came up with one of his stale jokes—"POP—CORN!"

158. **Jumbles:** FORGO BRAIN MANIAC OPIATE
Answer: Where did the old lady who lived in a shoe send her kids when they grew up?—TO "BOOT" CAMP

159. **Jumbles:** OPERA NUDGE JAUNTY GADFLY
Answer: What Dracula politely said, after enjoying his usual gustatory treats—"FANG" YOU

160. **Jumbles:** PAGAN CHESS GAINED PURITY
Answer: She said she was expecting to become engaged, because her boyfriend told her he'd give her this— A RING ONE NIGHT

161. **Jumbles:** FINITE MONKEY TWENTY PATCHY INFUSE ENGAGE
Answer: His new patented broom was such a success that it was this—SWEEPING THE NATION

162. **Jumbles:** PADDLE UNLESS SMOOTH ACCENT SORROW PLIGHT
Answer: The mall's new escalator had—ITS UPS AND DOWNS

163. **Jumbles:** EXCUSE BOUNTY HARDLY PILLOW ADVICE ACCEPT
Answer: If Marco Polo had needed money for his epic journey, he could have raised—ADVENTURE CAPITAL

164. **Jumbles:** GEYSER INFECT PICNIC MODEST HAIRDO VORTEX
Answer: The short movie he posted of himself catching a huge trout was a—STREAMING VIDEO

165. **Jumbles:** BLOTCH WALRUS UNFAIR DROWSY GASKET BISHOP
Answer: The Jumble cartoonist spent his vacation— WITH DRAWING

166. **Jumbles:** WISDOM MINGLE POTENT SHABBY ZENITH LOTION
Answer: The team's touchdown drive ended when they drove into a—NO PASSING ZONE

167. **Jumbles:** ISLAND STEREO INFANT ENCORE AROUND PURELY
Answer: After the Jumble puzzle maker said he was at a loss for words, he said—NO PUN INTENDED

168. **Jumbles:** NICELY UNLOCK SYMBOL BITTEN SICKEN OPPOSE
Answer: When Jones, Tork, Dolenz and Nesmith teamed up, everyone enjoyed their—"MONKEE" BUSINESS

169. **Jumbles:** EMBODY PULSAR RATHER PULPIT INVEST UPDATE
Answer: The enlisted soldier wanted to buy real estate, but he couldn't afford—PRIVATE PROPERTY

170. **Jumbles:** FIASCO BOTTLE UNSURE EMBLEM FEMALE HYPHEN
Answer: She couldn't find her husband in the casino. He went to play poker, but got—LOST IN THE SHUFFLE

171. **Jumbles:** UPWARD BOTHER SUBMIT MAINLY QUAINT CLOVER
Answer: What they called that much armed deep-sea bandit—"BILLY THE SQUID"

172. **Jumbles:** CROTCH TOTTER ZODIAC BABOON KETTLE VELLUM
Answer: What the bargain sale at the department store was—A "COUNTER ATTACK"

173. **Jumbles:** INFLUX DAHLIA SOCKET CELERY GLOOMY WINNOW
Answer: Where this form of exercise is popular—IN ALL WALKS OF LIFE

174. **Jumbles:** ESTATE BEACON FEWEST TYPING HEAVEN ADDUCE
Answer: A great composer involved with surgery— AN ANESTHETIC

175. **Jumbles:** MUSTER GOBLET PANTRY AVENUE DREDGE IMPEDE
Answer: What started as beef on the hoof ended up as this— THE LAST "GROUND-UP"

176. **Jumbles:** TREMOR RAGLAN MUSCLE BUREAU ISLAND MEADOW
Answer: If that snobbish horse is finicky about his hay, tell him you're serving this—GRASS A LA "MOWED"

177. **Jumbles:** BROOCH NICETY AUTHOR MENACE FAÇADE INVEST
Answer: Might help lengthen your life if you learn to do this—SHORTEN YOUR REACH

178. **Jumbles:** TALKER INVITE OPPOSE MARROW GUZZLE NAPKIN
Answer: What they gave the singer— THE "ZEAL" OF APPROVAL

179. **Jumbles:** ANYONE CEMENT PICNIC GHETTO MYSELF IMBIBE
Answer: "Will these steps take me to the Capitol?"— "NO, YOU HAVE TO CLIMB THEM"

180. **Jumbles:** FRUGAL BUTTER MORTAR ESTATE NIPPLE TROPHY
Answer: What there were when that pompous fool slipped on a banana—"PEELS" OF LAUGHTER